Home Church

"A Roadmap for the Worldwide Exodus Out of Traditional Church"

Terry Stanley

Home Church

"A Roadmap for the Worldwide Exodus Out of Traditional Church"

Terry Stanley

To order additional copies of this book or for more information,
visit us on the web at www.newtestamentchurchlife.com

Special thanks to Danielle Middleton
for her editing contributions

ISBN: 978-0-6151-7108-1
Copyright ©2007 Terry Stanley
Published by New Testament Church Life Publishing

Printed in the United States of America

To my fellow citizens and patriots in God's country who are scattered throughout the globe. To the hungry hearts who want more, who have not given up, who have held fast to the scriptures and who have known all along, that something is not quite right.

Contents

Good Morning

We are hungry for Jesus. We as Christians want more. We read the New Testament, and we see the way the early church lived. We see what the early believers had. And if we dare to be honest, we see that our experiences and practices don't quite line up with the New Testament example.

Sadly, the majority of Christians don't really see a problem with our current practice of "church" and Christianity as a whole. This is probably true for a few reasons. One reason is that most folks are not aware of anything different than what they are already practicing. People tend to accept what they are used to. People tend to think that what has always been practiced in their lifetime is right, correct, and normal.

Jesus aggressively spoke against the traditions of men. Yet today, Christians are "going to church" the same way their parents did, and the way their parents did before them, without taking an honest look at the Bible and what it says about the way we should be meeting.

It takes courage to be honest.

Jesus spent a lot of time rebuking the religious leaders of the day and their teachings. Still today, most people at large are doing just what the religious leaders of the day say we should do. Because a person goes to seminary and is now considered a "trained and credentialed professional", it does not mean their methods or ways are right.

In fact, **the role of the modern day church leader is found nowhere in scripture.**

We place more value on an intellectual mind than we do a broken heart. We respect education more than power. "The things that are highly esteemed among men are the things that God detests," (Luke 16:15). If a man today does not have a degree from a Bible college or seminary, he is considered not qualified to lead, yet Jesus used un-schooled fisherman to raise the dead and to establish the foundation of the church.

Our ways are backwards.

We assume that what is common, what is accepted, and what is widely practiced is officially correct.

Not so. There have been many times throughout history and in many cultures, when what was commonplace and widely practiced was absolutely horrible, yet everyone thought it was OK. This is true in our day and age in the church.

During this present day, there is very little being practiced in our church meetings that can be found in scripture, and we are suffering for it. We are currently in a "modern dark ages." We are in a time in which Christians everywhere have **accepted unbiblical practices to be the norm**. When the true Biblical concepts are read, concerning what should be our practice, everyone nods and agrees - in concept. But our destructive ways continue.

Christians are starving spiritually. Committed to "being fed" Sunday after Sunday, many Christians are spiritually impoverished and they don't even know it. We are used to eating crumbs. The modern day malnourished believer contributes to the making up of an entire church that is mostly powerless.

The church of the West has largely become a hybrid. The church has mixed with the world and the culture of the day. In many ways, we have accepted the ways of the world and have left the scriptural example. Because of the money and means we have here in America, we then propagate our hybrid ways to the rest of the planet and call it "mission work." We now have new believers in many parts of the world trying to mimic a church pattern of error we follow in America.

God will always love and bless His people. He is so kind and compassionate that he will give to us and even bless us in the midst of our ways. But there is a better way than our current practice - a Biblical way. There is a way that God intended which quickly grows and strengthens the disciple. There is a way that keeps families strong and brings honor to our King. There is a way in which would cause the world to marvel at the church, as it once did - and be drawn to it, rather than make fun of it.

The power and Spirit of the living God is within us. We have a clear example in the Bible of what to do and how to conduct ourselves. So what's the problem? Why are we not seeing the Biblical example being lived out in our day?

There are a lot of ideas out there. Since 1987, I have come across a variety of ways that people believe we are to *have church*. But when we look at the plain and simple direction of the New Testament, many of the ideas that are out and that are being practiced in traditional church settings and in many home gatherings simply don't match the examples of the scripture.

We as the church are a colony from heaven. We are to fervently love one another from the heart, and on a daily basis. We are to live and share life together. We are to be devoted to prayer and devoted to one another. We are to be filled with the Holy Spirit within ourselves individually and He is to fill our meeting rooms. We are to speak the truth to one another in love. We are to continually participate in our various functions and gifts, and not just in church meetings. We are to be truly "knit together" in heart. Vulnerable and transparent, in the Holy Spirit, we are to bear our souls to one another. We are to live a life of confessing our sins and weaknesses, bearing one another's burdens. Walking in the light and with intense accountability, we are all to be built up from the entire body.

We cannot be adequately fed from only one man, for only one hour, on only one day of the week. No matter how good of a man he may be.

The church of Jesus does not need money to run. Nor does it need a denomination (division) to be affiliated with. We do not need a building, a board of directors, an agenda, or a marketing plan in order to survive. But rather the Spirit of God, the power of the gospel, the love of the brethren and the authority of the scriptures are to drive our very existence.

We are to call no man leader, teacher or father (Matthew 23:8). For there is only One who is our Father and we are all brethren before our God. There is equality at the foot of the cross. From the crack house to the White House– all will stand before Jesus and bend the knee. Arrogant men, ambition, the need to have position, the need to have a title, and the need to be recognized as a "minister" or clergy has no place in the church of the living God.

We in the modern day church have sold out for what is flashy, for what is big, and for what makes a good show. The louder the music, the catchier the tune, the more people who attend now days makes for a "better worship experience." We are sending unseasoned people (mostly teenagers) out of the country on "mission trips" who are not living the life of Christ and won't share their faith with their next door neighbor. The thrill of going to another country to do missions seems to be more exciting than sharing our faith in the checkout line at the grocery store. We have resigned ourselves to shallow relationships, sitting on pews with people we don't really know, listening to an intellectual stimulating speech once a week, and farming our children out for somebody else to teach them the ways of God and of life. Godly sorrow, humility, and corporate prayer are all becoming rare commodities.

We should not be able to wait until the next time we can get together with our brothers and sisters. And when we do come together, we are to encounter the Spirit of the Living God. With Jesus in our midst, satisfying us, feeding us, speaking to us, filling us, encouraging us, and leading us, we are HIS BODY. Infused with His life, we are to be in sync with the head. "Membered" and planted with one another, we are to build each other up. We are to be a continual love feast in the Spirit of God, a safe place of growth, a home of strength and of security.

You have only one life to live. You've got one shot at this. And the time is short.

It's not too late. But it will take courage.

The job we have before us is a job of undoing. Hopefully, this book will be a source of direction - a guide for those of you who want something more.

If you find yourself defending your own experience while reading this, this book may not be for you. If you are satisfied with your current experience of church life and don't see what the big deal is, then my prayer is that these writings will arouse you from your sleep. Jesus and the church are not to be just a part of our lives but, the only life we've got.

The Purpose

There are vast numbers of Christians who are leaving the traditional church and seeking fresh ways to gather around Christ. For the most part this is a silent trend, but it is a strong one.

A recent Gallup poll concluded that each year 4,000 new churches start and 7,000 close. USA Today recently ran a story that said 1 in 4 young people (ages 18 - 30) have left the traditional church. In addition, 1 million people leave the traditional church each year, most of them young people.

The World Christian Encyclopedia recently estimated that there are already 112 million "out-of-church Christians" around the world. The study also noted that more than 20 million adults attend services in home churches each week. Recently, that number rose to 43 million.

In a report from the Barna Group, evangelical researcher George Barna said 70 million Americans regularly attend or have experimented with a house church - that's an increase of 8 percent since 1996. "The movement is taking on evidence of permanence," he said.

Especially with the younger generation, we are now questioning what is really genuine. We are asking "why do we do what we do" in Christianity. People are tired of lies. People are tired of hype. People are craving what is real.

An attempt to meet in simpler, more genuine ways is becoming the new thing. But the survival and the ability of these simple gatherings to thrive is yet another issue. Without an encounter of Jesus, we will be trading one dead form for another. We need to know what to do, how to do it, and how to undo what is not Biblical. There is a real shortage of experience available in this area. We don't need more concepts. We need practical truth, which is what this book is designed to provide.

Today, it is very clear that we would rather copy and rely on the traditions of men than the New Testament as a blue print. Unbiblical ways are ingrained in our thinking and in our culture.

Personally, I've had somewhat of an advantage. I wasn't raised in church. I had very few pre-conceived ideas of how the Christian life was supposed to be lived or what church should be like. When I read the New Testament for the first time in 87', it was very different from the church meetings I was currently attending. It became clear to me very early on that we were really practicing tradition, more than we were actually practicing what God's Word said. When I would ask pastors about simple things in the Bible in which we were actually doing the opposite, they would answer me with contrived and complicated answers. Something didn't seem right.

I was born again a Baptist church building in Houston Texas. Immediately after giving my whole life to Jesus, I wanted to tell the world about Him. I wanted to feed the hungry, give to the poor, and proclaim the good news. I saw everyone in the world in chains and bondage, and I wanted to set them free, just as I had been set free. I wanted the truth. I did not want to play games. I wanted to get together and talk about Jesus with other Christians, read the Bible, pray, and be accountable - and not just on Sundays, but all of the time. I read in the book of Acts how the New Testament church did the same thing. I thought it was amazing that I shared the same desires and experiences with people who had lived thousands of years ago.

But, how rare it was (and still is) for people to share these same desires today. People would tell me that they "didn't feel led," to go out and give of themselves. Most people only wanted to sit on a pew once a week for an hour and not get together any other time during the week. A deacon told me in 1988 that, "I was just a new believer and that the excitability would soon wear off." He said to me, "You will calm down after a while." That hasn't happened yet.

Within two years of my conversion in the Baptist building, I left my home in Houston, TX. and I headed off to college. I discovered in 1989 somewhere around 30 to 40 families meeting in different ways than the traditional setting. They were getting together in various houses, meeting in parks, meeting in rented community centers, and in many other ways. There was no one on staff, no designated official leaders, and no one was getting paid for anything. Leadership was organic and natural. Those who had gifts of leadership naturally lead. There weren't any schedules or bulletins. And it purposely didn't have a name - in order to cooperate with the New Testament example of there being only one church in any given city. However, we all met many times a week for meals, prayer, Bible study, worship, and fellowship. I'd never been exposed to such sincerity before. I was accidentally swallowed up into New Testament body life very soon after my conversion in 1987. I didn't read a book about it. But I began to live it and experience it. I learned about life in God at an extremely rapid pace. I was only 19 years old when I began.

There, during college, I found like minded and more importantly like hearted believers. I discovered people who, just like myself, held Jesus and the church as their WHOLE life. Not just a PART of their life. I soon married my wife Nanci. We now live in Bryan, TX where we are raising our four children, and continue to meet in non traditional ways with other families.

Without an artificial religious system in place which gives an appearance of keeping things going, what we have in non traditional gatherings can be very volatile. There is no sign out front to attract new members. There is no advertisement in the yellow pages to make us look established. We don't have big sound systems with entertaining rock and roll worship to make us look big and cool. All we have is the Spirit of God, a Bible, and each other. If in our meeting efforts we try to mix traditional systems and agendas with the Spirit of Jesus, it will quench Him and we will wither and die, or we will prop-up something that is dead and with no life.

As we attempt to get back to the basics of Christianity, it can be a challenging task due to years of traditional meetings ingrained in our thinking. Even in these new and simple gatherings, we will be tempted to rely on non Biblical methods to "keep the show going." We don't have to do this if we do what we ought to be doing in Biblical, New Testament body life.

Before we get into the nuts and bolts of the issues at hand, we have to establish some framework. We must understand the underlying reason for meeting outside of the traditional way. Some of the early chapters in the book do just that. They provide a new framework to build from. Therefore, parts of the early chapters can be somewhat theoretical, which I don't particularly like, but it is necessary. Therefore, some of the more difficult chapters to get through happen to be the first few, so be sure to hang in there until we get to more practical topics.

Throughout many chapters, I will attempt to weave in a variety of scenarios and examples so you can be exposed to several dynamics. It is always better to *see* the church, as opposed to only learning principles about it.

It must also be said upfront that some of the major points of this book include not only establishing how traditional meetings have actually hindered Christianity, but also how to move on and be successful in meeting and sharing life together in more Biblical ways. It will just so happen that as we attempt to do this, we will often find ourselves meeting in homes for the evening. As I often refer to "meetings in homes" in this book, I am not promoting a home church denomination. Any simple gathering, whether it be in a living room, outside in a park, or in any structure with four walls and a roof, is all the same thing. In other words, this book is not a push for home church only, although as we meet in New Testament ways, we will often find ourselves winding up in the living room.

The views expressed in this book are all subject to scripture. What I've written is based on the current light that I have and my current experience at this point in my journey. If anyone has a scriptural basis to challenge any idea in this book, I would deeply appreciate it if you would send me an email so that I may revise my thinking. At least, we could begin a dialogue together so that we could seek the truth together. The website, www.newtestamentchurchlife.com, has been revised and changed many times based on input and new light I've received from the church all over the world. Those who know me and walk with me are well aware that my views are always a work in progress and that the goal of my heart is to seek the truth. It is never my goal to be right and it is never to be critical. What I offer to you in this book is actually a collective experience of what works in New Testament church life. It's a culmination of my experience, the experience of my peers, and the older brothers who mentored me as a young man. I am inviting you the reader to join us in the on-going conversation of learning and seeking truth together.

I also really hope you hear my heart in these last few qualifying sentences. As you read this book, it will be evident that at times I am pretty tough on the roles of pastors and leadership, and on the traditional church. I will be the first to say that a critical spirit is never good, and I hope I do not come across that way. So while you are reading, please be aware that it is the methods and traditions that are the problems, and not usually the people. Most of the time, from my experience, pastors are quality men. Most pastors I've met are also very sincere. I've discovered that most people are really trying to do the best they can, and walk according to the light they have. However, it is our assumptions, our traditions, and the misunderstanding of roles that have caused so much destruction in the church today. It is not usually the people.

Why Going to Church

Is Not Biblical

There is nothing righteous about a building. There is also nothing righteous about a home or a living room. Most people agree that the building where people meet is not the church.

It's funny though how 99 out of 100 individuals will emphatically nod their head and say "Right, the building is not the church." But, then ten minutes later if you point to a religious building with a steeple on top and say, "What is that?" They'll say, "It's a church."

Jesus said, "*But the things that proceed out of the mouth come from the heart….,*" (Matt 15:18). Out of their mouths, all of the time people say, "We are going to CHURCH", or "Meet me at THE CHURCH," or "That's a CHURCH," – because THEY BELIEVE in their heart that it's A CHURCH. You might say, "C'mon, Terry, what's the big deal, it's just what we call it, we really know that the church is the people and not the building." I'm not so sure about that and I'll tell you why.

Our Words Represent Our Actions

Let's take a look at your average group of people who meet in a traditional church setting. They have services twice a week, Sundays and Wednesdays. They have a nice building they meet in. The building is outfitted with all the traditional markings. It has a sign out front with the name of the church. The sign contains a weekly, catchy, thought provoking phrase. The building has a steeple on the top. If not a steeple, then some other traditional looking top to make it look like a church. Inside, the building has long benches for the audience to sit on. It has a raised platform or stage at the front. It has a nice wooden box for an orator to give speeches from. Behind the speech making box and stage, there is a big bathtub which is raised higher than the stage.

While in this building, we are to conduct ourselves in a certain manner. There is special, extra reverent conduct expected from you as you are in this large meeting room. It is frowned upon anyone to eat or drink a beverage in this meeting room. This room is considered sanctified, which is why it is called the sanctuary - which means that this room is set apart or holy. This meeting room is viewed as though God Himself were living in it.

Let's do some experiments. Let's remove all the pews. Let's also remove the speech making box called the pulpit. All it is now is an empty room. How would this affect our meeting? Would it still seem like a church? Let's say we sat on lawn chairs and the preacher stood on top of a milk crate. Would it now still be a real church?

Let's say we took away the entire building. Let's say a tornado picked it up and moved it to Kansas. Now remember, we all agree that this building is not the church. But what if this building were obliterated? What would be the response of the people who met inside it? More importantly, what would be the emotional response of these people? Would they say, "*Our church* has been destroyed?" And if this building were gone, how would it affect their fellowship and their practice of meeting together? **Do we really believe that the church is really just the people?**

We all agree with **the concept** that the church is the people and not the building – but only in concept. If you were to take away, change, mess up, or alter people's **sacred building**, they won't really feel comfortable.

People associate the building, the pews, the pulpit, the steeple, the baptistery, a pastor – all those things are necessary with "having a real church." If you meet outside in a park, at 3:00 pm on Thursday instead of 10:45 am on Sunday, then you wouldn't have a "real church." If you baptized people in a lake or a river, instead of the bath tub behind the speech making stage, it would seem like the baptism was not quite as official or holy. In 1993, I baptized a man in a bird bath because it was all that was available. Was that baptism somehow less official than being baptized in a bathtub behind a pulpit on a Sunday morning at 10:45? In Acts Chapter 8, the Ethiopian Eunuch jumped out of his chariot and was baptized in some water right along side the road. The thief on the cross next to Jesus was never baptized at all, yet he entered into paradise. Perhaps we should consider if possibly God does not care about the things we care so deeply about.

"Well, Acts chapter 8 and the thief on the cross were during Bible times. Times have changed now", some might say. Sure, things have changed. But they have not changed for the better. Why do we think that doing things differently from scripture is all of a sudden now more correct?

When Jesus walked the earth, He met outside and taught people in the middle of tremendous disarray. There were people sitting down in the grass. There were people sitting in trees. Some people were probably on their way to the market with their livestock and saw the crowd listening to Jesus preach. They would stop to hear what Jesus was saying and had their cow or chicken there with them as they listened to the message. No one was dressed up in a formal way. When Jesus spoke, there were babies crying, people in filthy clothes, and people walking around toward the back of the crowd.

Was it considered a church meeting when Jesus would preach to the crowds? Of course it was! The church meetings throughout the New Testament include meetings outside, meetings around a fire, meetings in homes, and meetings in buildings. Paul was in a church meeting one time, and while he was teaching, a young man was sitting in a window sill. Imagine if during the next Sunday morning service somebody decided they couldn't hear as well from the back so they climbed up and sat in the nearest window sill? Someone would probably call security.

Here's the point. The building is not holy. But we believe it is. If you meet in a park, meet in a home, meet in a fancy Catholic building in Rome, meet in a tree house, it's all the same. Jesus said that "Where two or more are gathered together, there I am in the midst." Do we really believe that? C'mon, do we **REALLY** believe that?

Let's test it out. Could you meet with one other person, just one, on a Tuesday night in a park? You would read the Bible together, pray together, share hearts, worship God, and touch the Lord together. Would you consider that church? Be honest now… *would you still feel like you have to cover your God base by going to the official*

***church meeting on Sunday morning? Would you still feel
like you have to dress up, sit on a pew, and listen to a
sermon in order to feel like you've been in church?***

Our actions sometime betray our right Biblical concepts.

Our religiousity runs deep. It's all we've known, it's all we've
seen, it's all we've been taught. It's what we've believed for a long time
now…even though it is unbiblical. What about all the other things you
maybe unaware of that you believe and practice…. that may be
unbiblical? The Holy Spirit will help you. But it sometimes takes
tremendous honesty and courage to grow.

Why did the New Testament Christians meet in homes? It is
certainly not that a house is more righteous than a building. Once you see
and understand the essence of body life and what church really is, you
will see that THERE IS NO NEED FOR A BUILDING. In fact, it can
hinder and get in the way. Also, once your eyes are opened, you will stop
associating "being fed" with that of listing to a message once a week. The
New Testament Christians were not "fed" by a three point sermon once
a week by a paid professional.

What is the point of meeting together anyway? What is the
essence of the church meeting? The purpose is to touch the Lord, to
encounter Jesus, to be built up in faith, and to edify one another. When
this happens, He feeds us. He edifies the church. We are built up and
encouraged and He is blessed. The essence and point of the church
meeting is more easily accomplished as we keep it simple and don't
include all the extras and unnecessary practices.

It's Time to "Go To Family"

Many times in Christianity we use words or phrases which are not found in scripture. Phrases like "give your heart to Jesus, make a commitment to Christ, once saved always saved, loose your salvation, our church body, or the body of Christ here" - none of these phrases are found in the Bible.

Many times the idea behind such phrases was originally founded in scripture. But over time, we add to their meaning. Over long periods of time we create man made doctrines, and then we assume they are Biblical. *Assuming* that certain things are true without questioning them gets us into a lot of trouble in the church. Over time our words and phrases get packaged, re-packaged, and then packaged again. Many times the arguments and discussions we are having are not Biblical themselves. In other words, we are often asking the wrong questions. Or, the dilemmas we are trying to solve are based on assumptions that are in error themselves. Almost always, words and phrases we use that are not found in scripture are not scriptural ideas.

Huge ships are turned by very small rudders. Sometimes even the smallest error in our language (which reflects our thinking and our heart) can manifest itself with huge and consistent patterns of unbiblical practices in our lives. If you will learn to seek the Lord and examine the scriptures with no biases or assumptions, it will open a whole new world to you.

I would like to introduce to you another phrase not found in the Bible. Scripture never uses the words "go to church." And it doesn't use that phrase for a good reason. **You cannot go to something you are**.

The early Christians understood this. But we don't. Our lack of understanding in this area has caused severe and widespread damage. "But it's just words," you might say. If I said that God was a female, would you have a problem with those words? I would too. The words we use express what we really believe, and we live according to how we believe. Let's look at the absurdity of our practice of "going to church" and how it negatively affects our lives.

The word church in the Bible is the Greek word ekklesia. Ekklesia means "the called out ones." If you further study the word, you will observe some interesting meanings. The word also has with it the meanings of a family, a people, an assembly, or a council. It even has the idea of a modern town hall meeting for deliberation.

We could substitute the word "family" for the word "church". The church is a people. A family is a people.

Let's say that after a long day at work, you were heading home to eat supper and then retire for the evening. And, you were going to do this inside your house with your spouse and children. Would you say, "I'm going to family?" No you would not. You would say, "I'm going to be with my family."

Erroneously, church has become a function that we do on Sunday morning. Church has become an event instead of it being who we are. The word church has lost its meaning of family; the word has lost the meaning of us being a people. Going to church has become a weekly activity that we do. We've taken a word that defines who we are, a word that identifies us, and we've lessened it to an hour and a half episode that we do once a week. After the weekly church event, we then we all go home to our individual lives. It's like going to the theatre, or going to school, going to work, or going to the grocery store. "We're going to church!"

Look at it this way. If you **are** something, you **are** that thing everyday and you do what you **are** everyday. Are you a man? Then you never stop being one. Are you a woman? Then you never stop being a woman.

If you have kids then you **are** a parent. Do you ever stop being a parent? No. If you go to school, go to work, or you are at home, you are always a parent. You don't stop **being** a parent because of where you are or what activity you are doing. And here's the point: As a parent you should always be actively parenting. You should be praying for your kids while at work. You should be planning things for them, thinking about their needs even when you are not with them. When you are at work, you are working to provide for their needs, when you are home with them, you are actively engaged with them and interacting with them. If you are a parent, you are always a parent and you do at least some sort of parenting activity daily!

Same with the church! If we are the church, you never stop **being** the church. You cannot be the church on Sunday at 10:45 a.m. and then not be the church Tuesday at 10:45 a.m.

When we call the building a church or say that we are going to church we are practicing exactly what we are preaching, and we are living out exactly what we believe.

We have made something we are, into a weekly event. In some ways, I suppose it's perfectly appropriate for the church to meet in a commercialized modern building – because that's what we've done with the church. We've made it an impersonal, shallow, intellectual, 2 hour a week activity.

Erroneously, we have our life at work. We have our life at home. We have our life of activities. We have our life with our church. We have our life with our friends. It is all become separate and compartmentalized.

If God has saved you and you belong to Jesus Christ, then your new identity as a person is now with the church.

The church, corporately, is now who you are.

And you are to live the reality that you are the church 24 hours a day / 7 days a week.

We think growth as a Christian is learning more **about** the Lord, instead of ***knowing*** Him as a person. I can read a book all day long **<u>about</u>** who my wife is, but until I share her heart, and until I spend plenty of relationship time with her, I will not **<u>know</u>** her. Learning more information only teaches you ***about*** something. ***Experience*** is where true growth occurs.

In our day and time we know very little of intimacy. We know very little of how to be joined in heart and be truly knit together as a people of God, yet deep down, we all long for it. We have traded the intimacy of true church life for the falseness of an *institution*.

We are a living and breathing temple of living stones who encompass the true and living God. We are alive! Corporately, we are the very Bride of Christ. We are filled with the Holy Spirit, within and without. How offensive it is to call us a dead pile of brick and mortar. How it tells and exposes our lack of revelation of who we are, to say things like, "time to go to church." If we are not using New Testament language, it is because we lack revelation to some degree. If our beliefs are in error, our practice and what we live are in error as well.

Why You Can't

Legislate Intimacy

The best times are intimate times. We desire intimacy with the Lord. We desire to connect. We desire to share. We desire to be one with others. We also desire to share the Lord with one another in a close way.

When we structure it, it kills it. ***"The letter kills, but the Spirit gives life"***. The letter is the law. Structure, rules, agendas, bulletins, time schedules are all law oriented. These things kill intimacy through **legislation**.

Things of the heart are spontaneous. Things that are real and from the heart cannot be scheduled. "Ok, at exactly 2 pm, pour your heart out to Jesus, then stop it and shut it off when time is up." It doesn't work that way. When was the last time you organized and scheduled an inspiration? Or, when was the last time you planned when your next revelation would arrive? The heart is organic and made to flow.

When we get together as the church, the point of it is to have a very intimate time with the living God. We are to enjoy Him together. We are to love Him together. We are to love one another, pray for one another, and operate in our gifts as the Lord inspires us. As we are intimate with the Lord, it must flow and it must not be controlled –

otherwise we will offend the Lord and quench the Spirit, which happens way too often.

Man has continually tried to legislate intimacy over the years. Communism for example, doesn't work. You can't force people to hold all things in common and work for the greater good. I've heard of married couples pre-determining on which nights of the week they will come together. The vast majority of worship times are too scheduled, too structured, and too pre-determined in order to foster a natural and spontaneous flow. The way of *life* is spontaneity. Yesterday's manna is old stuff. Even if it was good yesterday, it's rotten today.

The best times I've had in any relationships have not been planned. We in the church are a long way from it, but I believe that if we were in love with Jesus all of the time, (and therefore loving one another often) we would be thrown into many daily church life situations in which we found ourselves preaching one another a sermon for instance, while working on the brakes on the car together; we would find ourselves singing praise songs on the way to the grocery store together; we would show up for a surprise visit at a family's house and wind up spending the evening in prayer and encouraging one another; we would find ourselves confessing sins to one another while sitting in the driveway in the car before we go in for the night.

Most things unplanned, we would be fed by Jesus all during the week by spontaneous meetings of body life. God should not be limited to a "Sunday morning" time, one hour a week to teach us, to use us, and to build us up. True church life in God is not to be "meeting-centered" but Christ centered – a spontaneous flow of love and unexpected blessings at unexpected times.

Life in Jesus and in the church is to be lived, not planned. Our hearts are not a water faucet to be turned on and off, but the very river of God flows through us, when and how He wishes.

An Organization

Or an Organism?

The church is alive. We are the Bride of Christ. We are Christ's Body. We are living stones. We are a living organism. The church must be left alone to be the organism it is and not made into an organization.

An organization is dead. An organization is like a business. An organization is legislated. An organization can be mapped out, written out, and planned out. It is something to be observed on a chalk board or in a text book. An ***organism*** on the other hand, is alive, evolving, unpredictable, ever changing, and constantly growing. An organism such as the church is not to be measured, contrived, pre-determined, calculated or controlled, but rather it is to be **lived and experienced.**

Let's look at a wild animal for example. Let's take an eagle.

An eagle can spread its wings and fly. It can fly wherever it wants to, it can fly how fast it wants to, and it can fly as high as it wants to fly. It can hunt whatever it wants to hunt. It can hunt when it wants to hunt and where it wants to hunt. This beautiful and organic creature can soar to the highest mountain tops. From the high mountain peaks, it can spot its prey hundreds of feet below and then dive with extreme accuracy to snatch its food from the tiny stream at the bottom.

What if we took this glorious and organic creature and put it in a cage? What if we provided its food for it so it wouldn't have to hunt anymore? That would be nice and helpful for the animal wouldn't it? And then, what if we scheduled when it was to eat? What if we also limited where it could go? Yes, in fact we shall build for it a big beautiful building to live in. It will be large, magnificent, and expensive. It will be such a beautiful *sanctuary*!

Perhaps organic things should not be allowed to roam so free and wild. We should contain them so they will have a proper diet, exercise, and environment to thrive in. We should even hire trained professionals to feed and care for the bird. Because of our modern wisdom and education, we've learned what is best for the eagle. We have become experts. The eagle will be much better off in our institutional care than in the care of its natural habitat.

In the above situation, would our eagle still be an eagle? Of course, technically it would still be an eagle. But it would not thrive. It would not live and be how it was intended to live and be. Soon, our magnificent eagle with wither, deteriorate and lose heart. It will not function properly as it should. And by our trying to help it, and enjoy it for ourselves, all we have done is helped it to weaken. Structuring and organizing a living organic thing will stifle it and it could even kill it.

The church is just like an eagle. We try to help it by containing it, packaging it, and over structuring it. We stifle its growth and cause people to lose heart.

Most people have never seen a wild eagle doing what it does in its natural habitat. We only read about wild eagles. The same is true for the church. Very few have ever seen the church functioning in its natural state and at its full potential. We only read about it in the New Testament.

It's because we've put the church in a cage.

What are some things that structure the living church **organism** and cause it to be an **organization?** And how does this man made structuring hinder and stifle us?

The churches in the New Testament did not have names. They were only referred to according to the city they were in. Giving a name to a group is probably the biggest thing that changes the church into an *organization* (refer to "One Church in a City"). With a name, we create an identity that is separate from others, thus we change the organism into an *organization*. A checking account, a church bulletin, a board of directors, by-laws, and documented membership lists are all things that create an organization. There are many more things that can do this as well.

Erroneously, there is a very strong need in men to legislate the church. Men want to identify it, categorize it, and organize it using modern Western ways. Instead of just allowing the living church organism to just be whatever it is, men want to be able to get their hands on it so it can be manipulated, easily identified, and managed.

Why can't we just *be people* who love Jesus and who are spending time together?

Our Need for an Organization

The answer is found in the words **security, having,** and being able to **count on** something. There is not much security in a lose network of Christians who are just spending lots of time together, without a name, without a building, without a regular meeting time, and without a membership list. Who would we be in such a case? What would our identity be? The answer is, we would simply be the people of God. Our name would be "the church of whatever city we happen to be in" (the church in Sacramento, the church in Pasadena, the church in Boston, etc.). Others would know who we are by our intense love for one another, our practice of close community living, and our constant good works. However, we have resorted to other, more modern ways to allow ourselves to know who we are, to let other people know who we are, and to be able to survive and increase our membership.

If you belong to a lose network of Christians who have no legislation, no identifiable name, and who are not an organization, you have nothing that your flesh can count on. With a loose network of relationships that is not packaged, branded, and boxed, there is not much of a feeling of having something you can control or belong to.

First of all, we must begin to understand that the church does not belong *to us*. Nor does it exist for us. It does not belong to a leader or to any men. **The church belongs to Jesus. We exist for Him.**

Men want to **have** something. Men want to **build** something. Many times, your pastor type people want to build their own kingdoms and say they are building God's Kingdom. If it were truly God's Kingdom they were building, they would do it His way and restrict themselves to only New Testament practices, and leave the building up to Jesus. Instead of being so concerned with growing it, building it, and managing it, men should **get their hands off the church**. If there is no membership list, no clearly identifiable line of those who belong to "us" and those who don't, then the people in leadership don't get to experience the feeling of having something to possess and build that is their own.

When we take the organic, living, spontaneous, relationship driven church and formally organize it, thus making it an organization, we kill much of the life and potential for growth. Groups ponder and question all the time how they can grow closer to one another, have more intimacy with one another, and have more spontaneity, yet they continue to depend on a modern *system of organization* to keep them together. Let me explain how this works and why it is so detrimental:

Cathy has a need. She needs someone in the church to help her do some yard work. In an **organization**, all she has to do is tell the pastor. He will then approve the need to go into the church bulletin. Anyone who wants to help can then be notified. On the surface, this would seem like a very efficient and effective method of communication. It maybe an efficient system of communication; however it will kill multiple opportunities for spontaneity, for relationships, and for intimacy.

Let's look how this particular need would be communicated and met with only a living **organism** of relationships, instead of an organization:

When Cathy feels the need for some help in doing the yard work, she picks up the phone and calls someone. Or, she can make a couple of visits in person to some people who are closest to her in her life. Cathy says to a family while standing in their kitchen, "Hey, I could really use some help with my yard. Could you all maybe find the time to help out sometime?"

What just happened in Cathy's situation? What does this personal, one-on-one asking accomplish when done in person? What does it accomplish, that a posting in a bulletin on Sunday, would not accomplish? It accomplishes plenty of things. If she communicates her need in person and through relationships only, Cathy gets to **have conversations** with people. She gets to ask with a vulnerable heart. She gets to stay over for 30 minutes and have a glass of tea. She gets prayed for. She gets to experience someone's heart on the other end of the conversation. The family that she asks gets to see her and hear her heart. They get to experience her real need as she communicates it as a real person. The people she asks gets to let Cathy know of some needs that they've been experiencing as well. The family she is asking also gets prayed for by Cathy. The family she is asking, in turn gets to ask Cathy if she will watch their kids while they go on a date for the evening.

ALL SORTS OF GREAT THINGS HAPPEN WHEN WE DEAL WITH ONE ANOTHER PERSON TO PERSON, FACE TO FACE, AND OFTEN.

Efficient systems and organization tend to separate us from one another. The church will have order, but it will evolve naturally from within.

Let's look at another example. It is Tuesday afternoon. John and Sharon are hungry for some fellowship. They would both really love to have people over to their house tonight. However, there is a scheduled meeting on the following night, which will be on Wednesday. They decide to go ahead and wait until Wednesday to get with people because in the church organization they belong to, they would have to notify the leadership and then announce the gathering at their house on the church website. Also, typically the way things work in their group, people like to plan things a week or so in advance.

Let's look at the same situation, but let's see how it might occur in only an *organism* or relationships, instead of an *organization:*

John and Sharon are feeling a need for some fellowship. John and Sharon would then pick up the phone and start making calls that very afternoon. The people they fellowship with are used to spontaneous invitations all of the time. Usually about half of the people they call will probably show up. Many will change their current plans or modify their plans, in order to be with the saints tonight. It doesn't matter to anyone that there is a regularly scheduled meeting the following night. Many acknowledge the Lord in the invitation.

Apparently, the Lord was really moving in John and Sharon when they felt the need to get the saints together on this particular Tuesday night. Sharon had a really big cry in her that she was unaware of because of some recent difficulties she was having at work. She really needed some counsel and some prayer. A new sister that no one had ever met before also showed up to John and Sharon's house that night. Several people ministered to the new sister with prayer and by talking through some things. The new sister would not have been able to make the Wednesday meeting on the following night. There was tremendous joy at John and Sharon's house that night because the people who came, came because they wanted to, not because they had to. Many were so blessed that John and Sharon would personally call them and invite them to their home.

Just think what it would be like if there were no formal man made organization, no system in place to take care of us, no fabricated structure for people to look to and depend on, nothing at all artificial to gather us together, to communicate needs, to make announcements, to tell us where to be, no organization to tell us who we are, when to pray, or when we could meet - but all that we had were *relationships* to accomplish all of these things. *How closely knit and intimate we would become!* Just think how many more spontaneous and intimate opportunities we would have to be joined together.

With only **relationships** to bring us together, what you wind up with is – **relationships**. With no organization to run the show and to automatically keep things going, you get prayed for and loved on much more often. There are also more real opportunities to serve and bless others. Intimacy, vulnerability and closeness come through much time and much person to person interaction. If we are relating to an organization instead of one another, it will contribute to keeping us apart.

An organization is an artificial method to keep us together and maintain continuity that ends up killing the life within.

Let's take another example.

Mark Griner is not in leadership in his church. However, Mark Griner loves to study the scriptures and he really has a heart for the growth of the other people in his fellowship. He is feeling stirred to share a teaching with the other members in his congregation. The Lord gave him this message only two days ago. He really senses that the other people he is with need to hear this message. He tells the leadership that he wants to share a message to the group. Since he is not a designated leader, the leadership wants to talk to him first in order to see if the message "fits with what the Lord is doing in the church". Really they want to screen the message (but they would never use the word "screen").

Because of scheduling conflicts, it takes about a week for the leader(s) to set up the meeting with Mr. Griner. About a week later they do get together and have a chat. The designated leader(s) feel like the message will be OK to share. (And, they don't want to say "no," because they don't want to be accused of being controlling.) Currently, because the leadership is in the middle of a teaching series, Mr. Griner needs to wait to share his message. Mr. Griner actually shares the message three weeks later. When it comes time for Mr. Griner to actually speak, the message is not quite as fresh in his heart as it used to be. He speaks mostly from memory of what the Lord *was* showing him almost a month ago, as opposed to what the Lord *is* showing him now. At the very moment he finished the message, the leadership stood up and took back control of the meeting. There were also a couple of subtle comments made by the leadership to the audience of how they disagreed on a minor point.

It was pretty clear to Mr. Griner that the leadership in the church was more or less "permitting" him to share the message, instead of really wanting and desiring him to share it. The way the whole thing came down and the vibe he got from the leadership was not extremely encouraging. In the future, Mr. Griner will not be quite as eager to dig in the scriptures in order to share teachings with the group.

Let's look at the same scenario, but within a New Testament environment. What if there were only a living organism of relationships to govern it and not an organization?

Mr. Mark Griner would feel stirred to preach a message to the saints. Immediately, he would bounce it off a few available brothers – any available brothers. He would then call the saints on the phone, or he would go visit each family to tell them about the teaching time and when it was. He would then share the message in a matter of days, full of the Spirit, with plenty of unction, in God's timing, and in total freedom.

Toward the end of the message, Mr. Griner felt impressed to pray for different people regarding the message he spoke. The message also inspired others to stand up and share testimonies. One young man stood up and confessed a sin. There was tremendous freedom and an atmosphere of healing in the group. Many were blessed and there were multiple breakthroughs that occurred.

Man's systems of organization dictate to us who is speaking, when they are speaking, and if they get to speak at all. The example of leadership we see in religious organizations is leadership by control, not facilitation. The gifts among us are often stifled and discouraged. In religious organizations, we are often given teachings on how we should be an active and functioning member. We are taught and encouraged to operate and function in our gifts, but then when we do, it is discouraged, frowned upon, or stifled.

Here's another example.

Frank Parker has a cousin coming to visit him from out of town. It's his younger cousin, Mark Parker. Mark just received his degree from Bible college. Mark is very excited to share his new knowledge he has learned in Bible college to a group of believers somewhere. Mark Parker asks his cousin Frank if he could share at the men's group meeting that Frank is regularly a part of. Frank asks his pastor if it is OK for Mark to speak at the men's meeting. Frank's pastor tells him "No, it probably wouldn't be best for Mark to speak at this time." Frank's pastor is personally aware that the Bible college cousin Mark graduated from is not really sound in doctrine. Conveniently, there are other things planned for the evening men's meeting anyway.

Let's look at this situation and how it would have came down within an organism of New Testament relationships only:

Cousin Mark shows up from out of town. He wants to share at the men's meeting Frank is a part of. He did not have to get permission. It is an open meeting. There was not even a designated person to get permission from. He begins to share at the meeting. He begins to share unsound doctrine. After he speaks for a while, an older brother in the meeting politely interrupts him. "Excuse me Mark. We sure do appreciate your willingness to share with us. But some of the points and topics you are covering are not exactly how the Lord has shown us to view and relate to those particular scriptures. In other words brother, your faith is not the same as ours concerning those issues. Would it be OK with you, if you and I talked about some of the topics you are bringing after the meeting time?" Cousin Mark replies, "Sir, what scriptures are you referring to specifically?" The older brother explains, "Well brother, again, would it be OK with you if we discussed it at a separate time?"

Cousin Mark finally gets the point. He humbles himself, agrees, and enjoys the rest of the meeting. Or, Cousin Mark may get offended, get real quite for a while, and then walk out of the meeting. The point is that everyone gets an opportunity to observe something, and to learn. The younger brothers felt protected by the older men. They don't need a system or a hierarchy to protect them, but **proper relating and functioning protects the church**. Cousin Mark gets a choice to be a humble man, to learn and to grow – or he can be offended – and everyone will get to learn by his bad example. Frank, Mark's older cousin, gets to humble himself as well. He gets to appreciate and respect the older brother who did such a good job of checking Mark. They grow closer in their relationship because of it.

In the above example, the identity of the group is strengthened. What they believe and the direction the Lord is taking them in is more affirmed, but not by an artificial system. In New Testament body life, there is no comparison as to the intimacy and closeness of relationships that you have, and the growth that occurs as opposed to when an organization is present. As I go and visit religious organizations, the people tend to be distant and separate from one another. They've been trained to be that way. There is a system in place that keeps them apart. A system or an organization is pure legislation. Legislation kills most spontaneity. Legislation stifles deep relationships. Legislation hinders many opportunities for growth.

"Yea, But..."

Some may say, "It is actually organization and legislation that brings us together and keeps us together. Without any organization, we would not ever meet or get together." This is probably true for many groups. If you drop your methods and systems of organization however, you will get to see what you really have. Without methods of organization in place, if no one gets together or pursues one another, you really didn't have much in the first place. People were probably coming out of obligation or religious reasons. The problem is that people *depend* and fall back on the system of organization to gather them together, provide teaching, provide music, provide activities and programs, and to keep out false teaching. This promotes passivity in the people. With no system in place to run things, it is up to *each member* to function and be active in heart – which brings more life, more growth, more learning, and much more quality. You have to risk the very thing you are afraid of.

Traditional churches are full of religious people who just want God's approval by belonging to the club and attending the club's meetings and functions. They don't really want true, meaningful, deep relationships with others, or with God. They just want to do the minimum requirements necessary to cover their base. If you remove the organization that **enables** them in this behavior, you will see what you really have. Jesus did things to expose the game players all of the time.

An organization tends to replace relationships. People relate to the organization rather than each other. People belong to the organization, instead of each other. People depend on the organization instead of only depending on each other. People give their money to the organization, instead of giving to each other. People invite others to be a part of their organization, instead of inviting others into their lives. People invest in and build up the organization, instead of investing in and building up one another.

The organization is often an idol, a "golden calf" in the hearts of its members. If you currently belong to a religious organization, it would be extremely rare to not hold at least some degree of affinity or allegiance in your heart towards your organization. If you threaten people's organization, or talk bad about it, the person who belongs to it feels threatened themselves. People have invested their time, their money, their hearts and their lives into building the organization. They do not know how to be, how to belong, or how to function with one another, apart from the organization.

Within an organization, members wonder and ponder how to have more intimacy with the Lord and with one another. So erroneously, they organize a meeting to be held in three weeks and post it in the church bulletin in order to discuss how to have more intimacy. We are addicted to systems. Systems that continually pull the rug right out from under us with what we are trying to accomplish in the first place.

While many are trying to pursue closer and deeper relationships with the Lord and with each other, because they belong to and are relating to an organization, it keeps them from being thrown together in spontaneous ways throughout the week.

Think about it like this. Imagine if you lived in a neighborhood of people with no cars, no phones, and no televisions. You would be forced to naturally relate to, talk to, and communicate with the people in your neighborhood. You would be dependant on one another in many ways for survival. This is currently a true situation for most villages on the planet. Just think how close you would become to the others who lived around you. You would have to get off your couch and go visit someone to borrow a cup of milk, instead of using the car. You would have to round up people and ask for help with various tasks and projects. In the evenings, you would tend to be together with your neighbors, sitting around visiting while watching the kids play, instead of watching TV by yourself in the evening. A few ladies might work together during the day to create meals for their families.

What do we currently have in our modern day and age? Instead of deep relationships with our neighbors, we don't really need anyone. We have cars, phones and televisions. Because of our lust for convenience and entertainment, these things have largely replaced the need for one another. Some may say that cars and phones have brought us closer together. But, cars and phones have only made us busier and more spread out. We probably know more people and have more relationships, because of the modern conveniences, but our many relationships are now much shallower and we spend less quality time with individuals. Without cars and phones, we would be stuck with just a few, but the quality and depth would be greater.

I am not against technology or modern conveniences. But, just like cars, phones, and televisions are conveniences that actually contribute to more shallow relationships and busier lives; we've done the same with the church. We believe that it is much more convenient and efficient to have systems of committees, schedules, bulletins, agendas, boards of directors, treasurers, CEO/ pastor, etc. We are convinced that these things help us, but they do not. We run the church like it was a business. This costs us the very thing we are trying to accomplish. Life together in Jesus! The typical church structure is not much different from a typical business structure you'll find in corporate America. If you compared say, Exxon's corporate structure with your average church organization, you would see some amazing similarities.

Again, in a New Testament, body life church, there *will be* organization. But it will happen naturally an organically. In a living organism of relationships, organizing can be done, but it will be accomplished through relationships and through personal interaction.

Forms Should Be Created From the Inside Out

I'm going to get a little theoretical here, but hang with me. It's important for our understanding.

We must always let the form of something take its shape from the life within itself. The form is never to be created first or sought after first. For example, an apple does not have the same form as an orange. An apple takes the form that it has because of the life within itself. It is in the DNA, if you will, of the apple that causes it to look like and take the outward form of an apple. The DNA of a banana causes it to take the outward form of a banana. Some bananas are a little bigger, some a little shorter, and some a little wider than others. The life that is within each banana causes it to take the shape that it does. The amount of nutrients it gets from the soil, the health of the banana tree it came from, and the amount of rainfall and sunshine all dictate the form the banana will take. The life within, causes the form to take the shape that it does.

The same is true of any living thing. Some dogs are bigger than others because some dogs receive a better diet, some get more exercise, and some have a different heredity. The life within causes the outward form to be whatever it is. ***The outward container becomes what it is, because that particular container happens to be what is needed to support the life within.***

The same should be true for the church. The church is a living organism. The life within it should cause its outward form to take shape. We should never predetermine the outward form ahead of time. It will kill and squelch what it would have turned out to be naturally. To assume upfront what something will look like will hinder it. To establish the form ahead of time will deny it of the natural form it would have taken otherwise.

For example, you may have ten families who are sharing life together in the Lord. Four families out of the ten, may need plenty of time getting to know other people because they are new and don't know anyone. Because of this, these four families will naturally and organically have it in their hearts to spend plenty of time visiting, talking and sharing with others. They may need many hours together telling stories from the past, asking questions of one another, and comparing notes on different subjects with one another. Three families out of the ten may already know each other well, but the Lord is leading them into a season of praying for personal needs for one another. They will want to get together to pray. They will not be talking together quite as much as the first four families are. Still, there may be a couple of families out of the ten who are really focusing outwardly with ministry and who want to spend a lot of their time together in order to help needy people in the community who need extra clothing and shoes.

Within these ten different families, the varying activities will look a certain way, if it is allowed to be what it is and not controlled. It will take a certain form naturally. There will be different nights of the week when various gatherings take place. Some will be for talking. Some will be for prayer. Some will be for sorting through clothing. There will be various get-togethers with a variety of emphasis. If you were to look at these ten families from the outside, the form and the way it looks will take its shape out of the various Spirit led activities that are happening.

The form will not be a cookie cutter form that is patterned after every traditional church organization on every corner in every city. That would be forcing something that is not natural or organically grown.

An organic form _allows_ the life within it to express itself in the most effective way it can. _**The form takes the shape that it does in order to allow the life within to express itself adequately.**_ If we were to pre-determine what nights of the week these ten families were to get together on and what they were to do when they got together, it would squelch the life and very little of what God would want to accomplish would ever be accomplished. In fact, as the Spirit brought up various things in the hearts of the families, they would tend to discount them because they would get used to not expressing the gifts they have.

An organic, natural flowing form takes it shape **because** of the needs of the people and **because** of the desires God puts in their hearts. Every group is different. Every season is different. There are different people in every group with different gifts, different needs, and who are all in different seasons. These things may change every few months. The needs and desires "from the inside out" should dictate the form and what it looks like.

An organic New Testament church lives from the inside out, not the outside in. If you dictate and legislate who gets together, when they get together and what they do when they get together, you will **kill** most of what could happen that would be so wonderful. Most Christians have never had the privilege of experiencing church life in a free flowing, uncontrolled setting.

Remember, even an extremely lose and well structured man made organization is still an organization. **Men must get their hands _completely off_ the church.** Let her be. Let her thrive and do what she does best. Let the Spirit of God dictate what the church looks like, in every city, in every gathering. The church belongs to Jesus. Let it take whatever form it **needs** to take. Let the needs of the members, the life within, and the passions within the hearts of the people form the structure. A healthy organism will grow and change. The structure must be allowed to grow, change and evolve with the organism. It will look different all of the time. Only a structure that is formed organically, will adequately support, carry and deliver the needs and direction the organism wants to go in.

Over the years, the people I've walked with have expressed themselves in various forms. It always looks different from season to season.

It is kind of hard to describe this. But for example, some months we have had a regular meeting time on Saturday night and a regular prayer time on Tuesdays. Everything else during the week was spontaneous. Then a few months later, we will shut down the Saturday meeting and have a Friday night meeting with an emphasis on worship and singing. Then after a while, when it seemed as though the Lord was finished with that, we would have no regular meetings at all for a few months. People will just gather together spontaneously. A brother might call a spontaneous one time teaching for a certain night of the week, a family may open their home for prayer on a particular night. We may all have a cookout with only a two days advance notice. There may be a ski trip planned with a four months notice. There may be a season where there are pockets of people gathering for different reasons. A few sisters may gather regularly to talk and pray together to learn how to love their kids better. A few men may gather together regularly to learn about finances. A couple of families may meet together to read and study a book together. All of this is sprinkled heavily with plenty of evening suppers together, lunches, and spontaneous prayer times.

There are a myriad of different forms that may take place if you allow the life within to dictate the form. Nothing is dead. No one comes because they have to. Nothing is religious. And no meeting is ever exactly the same.

Jesus said that He would build His church. Let's trust Him to do it the way He wants to.

Biblical Pastors

The word "pastor" is not in the New Testament very often. The word pastor simply means "shepherd." It is translated that way many times.

What does the Bible mean when it uses the word pastor? Although the word pastor is in the Bible,

The modern role and function of a pastor is found nowhere in scripture .

Our plague is that when we read a passage or see something in the Bible, we so often interpret it based on our prior experience or what we've already been taught. Based on prior experience, when we see the word pastor in the Bible, it floods our mind with our idea of what a pastor is – which is based on what we've seen, what we've heard, and what we've been taught a pastor **already** is.

If you had lived during the first century and then read the word "pastor" in a letter written to the church, you would have a much different idea come to mind.

What's the big deal? Why is this even an issue?

Our entire Christian culture has largely fit around this erroneous idea of this one man and his unscriptural role.

Entire groups and churches are built around the pastor. People join churches based on who the pastor is. The entire direction, vision, and focus of a group is often based on the pastor.

While the whole time, his role, function, and very existence are not Biblical.

We've been taught:

"If you don't have a pastor you are not under authority."

"If you don't have a pastor you don't have spiritual covering."

These are very common beliefs that stem from a basic error.

1 Samuel 10:19 *"But you have today rejected your God, who delivers you from all your calamities and your distresses; yet you have said, 'No, but set* **a king** *over us'."*

Just like the children of Israel cried out for a king, It is within the base nature of people to want a physical king. What does a king provide you? A king provides security. A king provides a feeling that someone is taking care of things and that someone is making decisions that need to be made.

The Catholics have their "fathers," the Protestants have their "pastors." People will always want someone else to take the responsibility off their shoulders. And we will even **pay** someone to do it. We want a specialist to take care of the role of leadership.

Men are responsible for leading the church. Not _a man_.

Our western culture has forced the church into that of a typical American, corporate structure. The modern day pastor has become the CEO of an organization, with the deacons acting as the board of directors.

We have reduced true shepherding to that of hiring a paid professional to stand up and make a speech once a week.

What is a real pastor?

What should true shepherding be? What should true shepherding look like?

A shepherd feeds sheep. A shepherd cares for sheep. A shepherd watches sheep. Remember, the word pastor literally means "shepherd."

To be a pastor is to be a shepherd. To do the work of shepherding is to speak into the lives of others. To shepherd is to watch over the lives of others. To shepherd is to care for the well being of others, (Lk.2:8, Heb. 13:17).

The Greek word for shepherd is poimaino {poy-mah'-ee-no} which means to feed, to keep, to tend, to care for, or to shepherd.

1Peter 5:1-4 *Therefore, I exhort the* **elders** *among you, as your fellow elder and witness of the sufferings of Christ, and a partaker also of the glory that is to be revealed, shepherd the flock of God among you, exercising oversight not under compulsion, but voluntarily, according to the will of God; and not for sordid gain, but with eagerness; nor yet as lording it over those allotted to your charge, but proving to be examples to the flock. And when the Chief Shepherd appears, you will receive the unfading crown of glory.*

Notice that in the passage he writes it to elders (plural) that are among you. Peter told the older brothers to do the shepherding. From Peter's perspective, there are **many** among us who will be doing the work or feeding the flock! Peter is simply telling the elders to care for the younger members.

In a healthy group of Christians, we should see many people doing shepherding.

While on the earth, and as a man, Jesus Himself actively shepherded twelve men. He spoke into their lives. As a man, He lived close enough with them to see their lives and address them. If Jesus shepherded twelve, why do we think that one man among us can adequately shepherd five hundred people?

Maybe a man among us can shepherd one hundred people?

No.

Well maybe fifty?

Nope.

He can't.

If Jesus had twelve, we would be doing very well to adequately shepherd just a few.

A man **can** stand up and give a teaching week after week to 500 people. But he can not shepherd them.

How should shepherding really occur?

Like this:

As you are meeting with the Church, living life together, and loving the Lord together, it may come up in you or in somebody's heart:

- To be interested in the well being of another saint or even a few.

- To become genuinely interested and concerned for a few people's growth and life in God.

- To regularly pray for them, look at their lives and consider areas of growth that may be needed.

- You will probably pull these folks aside spend time with them, provide instruction, encouragement, and love by speaking into their lives on a regular basis.

Someone who is doing shepherding does not necessarily have the gift of teaching, although he should be able to teach (1 Tim. 3:2). You can carry someone in prayer, speak into their life, and care for their growth in an active participatory manner, without having the gift of teaching. The church has often called "pastors", those who only have a gift for teaching.

A shepherd can often care for and be concerned with the growth of a larger group. He may even stand up and teach on occasion to the group as to what the Lord may be saying for growth or issues of correction or vision, but this is in no way a weekly thing. It may be for three nights in a row. It may be once every month or two. It may be a one time thing.

Keep in mind that in the body, someone doing shepherding is a sheep themselves. They are not to be considered in a different class or "above" anyone else. It is just a function they are performing, like teaching or prophesying.

Someone that is doing the work of a shepherd will probably be older, but not necessarily. Notice that Peter seems to make synonymous the function of shepherding with exercising oversight and being an elder in 1 Pet. 5:1-4.

In the church today, we have severely changed the role of a pastor and what shepherding is all about. We've made men hirelings. When you pay a man a salary for giving a speech once or twice a week, and call it shepherding, it does all sorts of terrible things.

First of all when you pay a man a salary, it tempts him. What if he doesn't perform? What if he is not inspired one week? What if he is dry in his heart and life and needs prayer and for someone else to take the ball? What if he needs to stay home Sunday morning because he hasn't had much family time? He can't. His livelihood is on the line. He's getting paid for it! It becomes a job. He **must** perform.

The modern day pastor has become the planner of events, one who delegates, and an organizer of committees. He becomes spread so thin with his time and emotional energy that he gets burned out and often loses his inspiration. This man is obligated to fill his role or he will be fired and will lose his pay.

He also has to maintain somewhat of an illusion of not having problems. He can confess some things to a certain level, and probably does to maintain some perception of humility, but if he were ever to be really gut-level honest with anyone, it would scare the congregation and cause mass panic. Therefore, he becomes **cheated** of true body life.

Usually, he is the loneliest man in the fellowship.

The modern day pastor's family suffers. His children are often rebellious, because they are the product of a failed system. The family is sacrificed because the pastor often doesn't have time for them. But even worse is the hypocrisy. Again, because he's "the pastor," he and his family have to maintain an illusion, a veneer of righteousness, when they are really not. At home, all sorts of stuff goes on, just like in any family. But around the church members *the act* is turned on. This puts emotional pressure on the family and a feeling of being false. This is very damaging.

Pastors Hinder Our Growth

In 1 Cor. 14:26 we read, *"What is the outcome then, brethren? When you assemble, each one has a psalm, has a teaching, has a revelation, has a tongue, has an interpretation. Let all things be done for edification."*

The modern day pastor also stifles the growth of the church. His role on Sunday morning doesn't allow us to hear from the rest of the body in the general assembly. This limits our experience of what the Lord would want to say through the other members.

But worse than that, the pastor's role on Sunday causes others to sit passively in the pew as observers and not as participants. As a member of the modern day church, you are allowed to show up and hide if you want to. You can be needy and desperate in your heart on Sunday morning - go to the church meeting, listen to the sermon, go home, and nobody would know the difference. Many people Sunday after Sunday are dying inside, hurting and alone, just sitting on the pew. They come with hope in their hearts that someone will notice and again they leave disappointed. This will happen this coming Sunday in countless gatherings all across the country.

On Sunday morning, you can be in a bad place in your heart and know one will know it. You can be full of the Spirit and no one will know it. Sometimes, the best time on Sunday is usually the 10 minutes before and after the sermon, when you get to visit and connect with others.

We should never go to a church meeting and leave unchanged. Every time we get together we should leave filled, listened to, prayed for, and even more connected with Jesus and others.

Since I've become a Christian, I've known about 4 real pastors. I've known many who have the title of "pastor", but they don't do true shepherding whatsoever. **Often these are quality men**, but their real gifting is more in things like administration, teaching, or music. Some of them have a strong gift of "helps", but they have been misidentified as being pastors.

Just because a man has started a fellowship or was an original founder, it does not make him a pastor. Just because a man is eager, knows the word of God, can teach, attends seminary, or has leadership abilities – none of these things cause him to have the gift of a true pastor. Please don't miss my heart. I do not intend to speak down to or degrade these men at all, but in most cases shepherding is just not their gift.

Most of the so called pastors I've known, know nothing of hospitality, which disqualifies them from being in leadership (refer to chapter on hospitality). In addition, most of the so-called pastors I've known will never ask anyone about the condition of their heart or how they are doing in their faith. A lot of these men are pretty self-focused (but they would never think they are). And most of them have no idea of what the scripture means when it says that "Jesus, *seeing* the multitudes felt compassion." It takes a pastoral gift from God to regularly and in daily life be *seeing* others with compassion. Again, these are usually good men, but most of the time, they are not pastors – at all. Usually, if they do spend time with you, it is either to protect the organization they've built or grow it in order to add to its numbers.

Only the rare and true gift of a shepherd will be genuinely interested in you and who you are, and on a continual basis.

Spiritual Authority

There is a tremendous difference in spiritual authority and authority that is given a man because everyone agrees on his authority. Spiritual authority comes from the Spirit and from the Word of God. You *just are* a pastor, because of your heart and the gift of God in you. It cannot be learned from seminary, and you don't receive it automatically because you started a church. We have an extremely damaging system of authority in the church today. It hinders people who have gifts from God and true authority from the Spirit. The only gifts of leadership that are recognized are those "on staff". In other words, if you are not on staff, then you don't have as much authority, if any, as the ones who are on staff. We should be able to publicly recognize spiritual gifted people among us, without it being a paid *staff position.*

The problem is that there are many people in traditional groups who are gifted, who have tremendous weight, spiritual authority, and leadership authority who go unrecognized and unnoticed because they are not staff members. This hinders the growth of the church, promotes frustration, and ultimately passivity in the group. Many times, the only outlet for these gifted people to express the gifts that are in them is to go start **another church**, therefore establishing themselves in a leadership position. If we would publicly recognize those with leadership gifts and authority among us, it would vastly cut down on the number of divisions in each city.

There is usually a consistent identity problem in most pastors or men in leadership. Usually from the ones who attend seminary, they think of themselves… "as pastors." They don't see themselves as just another brother, but inside of themselves, they are in a different class than the rest of the sheep. It's part of the clergy/laity separation which is false and it's how they've been trained to think of themselves. Part of this identity problem is that the church is **their baby**. Subtly, they forget that the church belongs to Jesus, not to men and that He is the one who is building it. Anything that threatens the organization they have built will usually solicit extreme emotional reactions in these brothers. This identity problem is very hard to shake and they are usually very reluctant to become just brothers, yet still function in their gifts. All they've believed, all they were trained for, all they've built, their place in society, their entire identity would come crashing down. Actually, the ones I have seen let go of their pastor identity are very relieved once they do so, and they begin to thrive more than ever in their gifts and functions.

In their hearts and before the group they are with, the "pastors" need to resign. They need to find work, and they need to become just brothers in the church. Then if they truly have a gift of shepherding they can do still do it, but from freedom, and do a much better job.

Offices, Titles, and Gifts

Men love titles. Men love position. Men love status. People love men of status. People love the illusion of security that comes with men having titles among them. These things have been abused in the church. This is obvious to most people. But why? And more importantly, what can we do to correct it and how can we relate to these truths in a healthy way?

Offices

First of all, our modern idea of an "office" is not a Biblical one. The Bible was not written in Dallas, TX. We've tried to interpret and apply Eastern ideas in a Western culture. When we read about offices, we interpret it as being the same as someone who has a management position in corporate America.

A Biblical office is not the same as having a title, a business card, a sign on your desk, and a salary with benefits. We cannot forget that the church is alive. She is a living organism and the church is relational. Hopefully in this chapter, we will see gifts, titles, and offices the Bible speaks of, are much different than what we've made them to be.

The word office simply means the "function of" or the "work of." In 1 Timothy 3:1 the phrase "office of a bishop" comes from one

Greek word. The one Greek word is episcope. It simply means *to do* overseeing or *to do the work of* an overseer. ..."If a man desires the office of a bishop, he desireth a good work." All this is saying is that if you want to help others in their lives by watching out for them and helping them in their growth, then that's a good thing to do. But when we typically read that verse, it runs through our filter of our Western culture. Read the verse again. When you read the word "office" this time, think of the word as "doing a work," because that's what the word means. A Biblical office is more of **a description of activity**, as opposed to a title.

Next, we see the word "office" again in 1 Tim. 3:10, 13. Here it is used in conjunction with the work of a servant or "deacon." The phrase "office of a deacon" is the one Greek word, diakoneo. To be a deacon is to be a servant or to do the work of a servant, or "to wait upon." If you serve someone in the church then you have just entered into the office of a deacon. Remember, the word office is a description of activity. To be a deacon is not to have a position; it just means that you are doing the work of serving others on a consistent basis.

In Acts Ch 6, the church was brand new in Jerusalem. Thousands of new believers were hanging out together, listening to teachings, and eating together. In chapter 6, verse 1 of Acts, we see that there were some widows who were not getting served food at the daily gatherings. They were being looked over. Now that could cause some real hurt feelings! What did the church do about it? The whole congregation chose 7 guys who were filled with the Holy Spirit, of good reputation, and who had wisdom to remedy this situation. Note that the same word for deacon, "diakoneo", in 1 Tim. 3 is used here in Acts 6 as well. **These 7 men entered into the office of a deacon.** Or, to not be religious about it, we could just say that they were doing some serving. But why the big deal about who did the serving? Why did they have to be filled with the Spirit? Why did they need wisdom and have a good reputation just to hand out food? Why did the apostles lay their hands on them just to serve some tables?

In our day and age, we would probably choose any brother just to serve a few tables. "Hey Joe, grab a few of those teenagers over there and pass out that food would ya? The widows are getting a little upset 'cause they didn't get their ham sandwiches."

Be aware that the same qualifications for doing serving found in 1 Tim 3 (office of a deacon), are the same qualifications that the 7 men had in Acts Ch 6. Same function - serving. Why the qualifications for serving? Well, look at the results.

Immediately after the passage about waiting on tables it says in verse 7 that "the Word of God kept spreading and the number of disciples continued to increase…"

Wow! Then in verse 8 it tells us more about Stephen. In verse 8, "Stephen full of grace and power was performing great wonders and signs among the people." Remember? He was one of the guys that was waiting on tables!

The point is that the men who were serving tables were **among the people**. They were with the people, mixing up with them, speaking to them, and loving them. Passing out the food was a great opportunity to speak, love, pray with people, and to serve. That's why anyone wanting to serve (do deacon work) should have a strong relationship with God. Because when we serve, it is an opportunity to increase the Kingdom.

Someone who is serving half-heartedly not filled with the Spirit will eventually complain about it. Sooner or later they'll have a bad attitude and not represent Christ at all.

I Timothy Chapter three provides us a list of character qualities for people who are wanting to watch others lives or who is wanting to do serving.

In this passage, Paul tells Timothy that they need to be living right, not addicted to wine, managing their own household well, etc. This is important because anyone who is serving or leading has a tremendous opportunity o advance the Kingdom, just like the brothers in Acts who were waiting tables. Their character should be of good quality. Let's look at a common error however, that is made concerning those character qualities.

"Blameless." This is the Greek word anepileptos. It simply means there is nothing in your life that needs a rebuke. It doesn't mean that this man has never committed sin. That would disqualify everyone. It simply means that you are living a right and clean life with God. To be above reproach or blameless simply means that you are not walking in sin. Past sins can not disqualify anyone from leading out, serving, or helping others because then no one could ever be qualified to do it. If it is in your heart to help others in the church in such a way that you are watching their lives and helping in their growth, then you must have your own life working well and not be walking in sin.

Gifts Are to be Observed, Not Filled.

Again, the church is organic and alive. We should never force anything. We are not to try to find people to fill positions. We are not to see the lists in scripture of the various gifts and functions, and then try to fill those job positions. We see in scripture that there are teachers, prophets, shepherds, evangelists, apostles, deacons, administrations, helps, etc. We should not shop the list by saying, "Ok, we need a prophet. Who is going to be our prophet? Now, we need an evangelist. Who is going to be our evangelist? We need a shepherd. Who is going to fill the role of shepherd among us?"

These gifts and various functions are to ***naturally evolve and just organically operate*** among us. A person's gift is, whatever it is. If a person naturally functions in the gift of evangelism, then we might say that he is an evangelist. If a person operates in the gift of the prophetic, then over time, we might say it looks like he or she may be a prophet. If a person naturally functions in shepherding, then we might say that they are a shepherd. We don't go out and try to find a shepherd. And we certainly are not to conduct job interviews and hire a shepherd.

Let's briefly look at Titus Chapter 1. In verse 5, *"For this reason I left you in Crete, that you might set in order what remains, and appoint elders in every city as I directed you, namely if any man be above reproach, the husband of one wife, having children who believe, not accused of dissipation or rebellion. For the overseer must be above approach as God's steward, not self-willed not quick tempered, not addicted to wine, not pugnacious, not fond of sordid gain, but hospitable, loving what is good, sensible, just, devout, self—controlled, holding fast the faithful word which is in accordance with the teaching, that he may be able both to exhort in sound doctrine and to refute those who contradict."*

This is a great passage. Paul told Titus, who was in Crete, to appoint elders in every city. Who should Titus appoint as elders? **Those who were already elders!** He didn't make them elders. He just recognized them publicly. They already had the qualifications within themselves.

Look at the word "namely" that Paul uses in the first sentence. If you will read that word with understanding, you will see that Titus was to just publicly recognize what ***already was***. Those who already were elders, the seasoned brothers who could do overseeing effectively were to be pointed out. He was not to groom men for a position. They were not to take a six week training course. He was not to run an ad in the paper. He was not to conduct interviews. He was not to form an elder search committee. The elders were already there in the midst of the people. They already had the qualifications evident in their lives, they just needed to be pointed out. The list of qualifications Paul gave was just to help Titus recognize them and find them from among the people. Notice also that the qualifications for overseeing or eldership have nothing to do with having education. It's all character.

Whatever gifts happen to be among us, simply happen to be among us. One particular group may not have anyone who functions as an evangelist much. You may not have any apostles among you. You may not have someone who functions primarily as a prophet. That's OK. Don't try to create one. If your numbers are small, you will not have all the gifts and functions among you. But you will have some. As more people begin to come around, you will observe more gifts and functions operating in different members.

You cannot learn how to be an evangelist. You either are one or you are not one. You can't go to school to become a pastor. You either have that kind of heart or you don't. These gifts are from God, they are not skills to be learned. You cannot study and then become a prophet. You either have a gift from God or you don't. These are supernatural, spiritual gifts. As you mature in Christ, your gifts will become more potent or fine tuned, but you can't take a course and become a gift to the church.

You the reader, have gifts, right now from God that He gave you to edify the church. Today, there is a real over emphasis in the church to "know what your gifts are." There is no need to take a personality profile test to discover your gifts. As you are abiding in Jesus and filled with the Spirit of God, your gifts will come to the surface and you will naturally function in them. You will know what your gifts are as you and others **observe** how the Lord is using you and has used you in the past. Don't sit in a living room together and say, "you're a this and you're a that." Christians are often labeling themselves according to personality types, and there is no profit in it. The overemphasis in the church today to know what different people's gifts are largely stems from self focused, humanistic, feel good psychology.

Having a focus on labeling ourselves with gifts does not help us be more of what we already are. It only trips us up in trying to fulfill something that we think we should be fulfilling. We need to keep our eyes on Jesus. And we need to keep our eyes on the cross.

We don't even fully know the full definition of the various gifts. Over the centuries, we've modified them, interpreted them, categorized them and canned them. Just look at what we've done with the gift of shepherding.

Looking at another example, an evangelist is listed as a gift to the church. Our modern day definition of an evangelist is someone who converts lost people to the faith. The word means "bringer of good news." What if an evangelist really is a gift to *the church*, as it is stated in the New Testament? A true evangelist may be someone in the church who is always sharing good news with not only unbelievers, but with Christians as well. There is a tremendous benefit from encouraging other Christians with various messages of the good news of God, even if they are already saved. We as Christians really need good news all the time. Could we be limiting or even missing the true gift of an evangelist by defining him and categorizing him as we tend to do?

We have so many assumptions, that we would do better to not focus on what our gifts are so much and then try to fulfill them, when we may be working from an erroneous model in the first place. **We are whatever we are**. Let's let the gifts that we have, organically **define themselves**. Our identity is in Christ, not the labels or gifts we are to the church.

An apple tree makes apples because *it is* an apple tree. Apple trees don't learn that they are apple trees, and then start producing apples.

The School of Life

As individual Christians, how do we grow? How do people in general grow? How does a plant or a tree grow? How do children learn? How did you learn to swim? How do you learn to have a good marriage? How do we learn to raise kids?

I'm not talking about gaining head knowledge. I'm not talking about the ability to regurgitate information. I'm talking about true growth. How do we get those things in us that no one can take away? How do we truly learn the lessons in life that are now rock solid in us? How do we arrive at things that are unshakeable? How do we gain those precious gems in our character that remain forever? One word.

Struggle.

The way of true growth is through struggle. The way of true growth is by pain. Sorry, but there is no way around it. You can hear teachings all day long about how you need to cry out to God - but unless you *feel the pain,* you will not really be crying out. You can hear a teaching or read a book about how you need to be broken, but unless God breaks you, you will still have some form of ambition and self reliance.

Brother Prem Pradhan, an apostle to Nepal, told me in 1992 that growth comes only through suffering. I didn't believe him. I thought I could grow by learning. I thought I would grow if I got all my questions answered. Not true. There is no formula for growth. There is no formula for the growth of the church either. We grow when we are brought down to nothing. If we are not experiencing Christ in a certain area of our life, God will allow us to be laid waste in that area until we learn to cry out to

Him. Only in the person of Jesus Christ will we find the secret to the Christian life. How is this related to our chapter title of gifts, offices and titles? Keep reading.

The Absence of Dominant Men Builds a Strong Church

During Paul's missionary journeys, he entered a town, preached the gospel, stayed a while, and then he left. After the early churches were planted, the apostles left them shortly afterwards. They did not recognize elders in those cities until much later. Sometimes it was months, sometimes it was years later until elders were even recognized. It was Paul's habit to appoint elders during his *second* time through a town. We even see in Titus 1:5-9 Paul instructing Titus to recognize elders in Crete. This is after the Jews accepted Christ in Crete from the preaching of Peter years before.

After the apostles preached the word and left town, the new believers in that city only had the Lord Jesus and each other. They didn't even have a New Testament. It had not been written yet. Paul's letters came much later. How did the early churches survive without Paul staying with them? How did they survive with no leadership in place? How did they survive without a local strong leader present? Very well. They changed the course of history.

When Paul, Barnabas, and Silas preached the gospel to a town, they left it with no leadership in place because it was necessary for the church to not depend on anyone. That was the best way for them to grow and to learn how to function. You cannot learn to stand on your own two feet, unless you are required to do so. This is true both individually and corporately. If Paul would have planted the church in a city and then stayed there, they would have become dependant on Paul. They would not have become strong. They would not have thrived the way they did if Paul would have stayed for years and taught them many messages a week. Teachings and messages don't grow us. They can only point us in the right direction.

The absence of dominant men builds a strong church. Once the foundations are established of a functioning and active church, then the church can properly relate to and continue to function with strong brothers present. This is why those who lead should slowly and naturally evolve from among the group itself. This is why Paul recognized those who were elders only **after** the church had time to become rooted. If strong leaders are established right away, then everyone shuts down and defers – which is what we have in the church today.

The best thing for a new group of believers is to be told the truth, pointed to Jesus and then be left to themselves to learn how to need Christ, learn how to do their share, learn how to pull their own weight in the church, and learn how to need one another. This is a crucial time when essential foundations are laid. From among this assembly of strong fellowship and intense love for one another, then and only then should organic, naturally occurring plural leadership arise and over time be recognized.

Because of our misapplication of leaders among us, we have become addicted to men leading us, instead of being addicted to Christ. We have become addicted to only certain people functioning, instead of everyone learning to function for the very survival of the group. We have become completely accustomed to a certain few taking the responsibility for the church, when we should all have equal responsibility. We will only learn to rise to the occasion, hold fast to one another, and become a strong church if we have no one else to do it for us.

The Essence of Church Life

Years of living life in this fallen world have taught us that life on this planet is not a real safe place. As we are vulnerable with fallible and mistaken parents and siblings, we learn very early we **will** be hurt. We **will** be hated. We **will** be ridiculed. We **will** be left alone and abandoned. It's inevitable. As children, very early on, we learn to self-protect by putting up walls around our hearts. We've all done this to some degree. We learn to cope, to live through it, and to get by in life so it doesn't hurt quite so much anymore. In short, we learn to live self protected and self guarded.

Self-protection and self-preservation are very natural responses to a world full of trouble. With our walls of self protection, we are able to function, to have jobs, to raise kids, to pay the bills, to relate to people. But our walls of self preservation have a cost as well. We don't really get to live in true freedom - freedom from the heart. Sure, we can get along with others and be functioning human beings in society, but haven't you noticed? Many people, I'd say most people, have become as though they are walking dead people.

Many are just getting by. Many are just surviving. Merely going to work everyday and going through the motions of life. Almost robotic, instead of *feeling* the pain of rejection, *feeling* the pain of being hated, *feeling* the deep loneliness, we choose to mostly *feel nothing* at all.

There are a myriad of reasons why people are the way they are: tendencies that stem from heredity, various flesh patterns that we've developed to cope with life and to self-protect. But the bottom line is all the same...

Jesus wants to heal us.

He wants to restore to us the lost years. He wants to make you healthy inside and out. He wants you to be alive from within. He wants you full of passion, full of love and full of purpose. Jesus wants you to be free in your heart and in all of life. He wants you filled with His power and bearing fruit 100 fold for the Kingdom. He wants to use you to give to others as well. What is His plan and design to heal and restore all of us messed up human beings?

When you were born-again, you were healed. But we don't always experience the healing we have. There is a process of renewing our minds and a process of sanctification that allows the Christian to experience more and more healing and restoration. God wants to restore us from two directions. Not only is He going to heal you and renew your mind as you continue to relate to Him directly as an individual, but He wants to also use *a functioning and active church* to restore you and build you up as well. Both are important.

Knowing "About" versus Knowing

As we truly know the Lord as a person, we are changed. As opposed to just knowing and learning things **about** Him, as we are truly **knowing** Him, real change in the heart occurs.

It's like the difference between reading a book *about* skydiving and actually skydiving. Reading a book only fills your head with concepts *about* skydiving. When you actually skydive, you *know* what skydiving is really like. Concepts can be dangerous. If we don't put concepts into practice, they can fool us into thinking that we have the *reality* of the matter, when we really only know things *about* it.

Concepts *about* the Lord do little to change our lives. *Knowing* the Lord is what changes us. We must never be fooled between the difference of knowing things about the Lord and actually knowing Him. Learning *about*, is obtaining more information. Knowing Him however, is actually tasting and experiencing who He is.

As we go deeper in really knowing the Lord, the walls in our hearts begin to come down. We discover that the Lord Himself really is a safe place to let our guard down, and that we will not be hurt by God or destroyed. We experience the relief that comes from finally being loved by someone who loves us no matter what. And, as our relationships with others are truly in the light and in the Spirit of God, we learn to have this wonderful vulnerability with one another – loving one another fervently from the heart.

You must understand that you are like a plant. You are a plant that the Lord has grown and is continuing to grow. He put His seed in the soil of your heart. And, so far as you've been cooperative, you've proven to be pretty good soil.

The Lord can and will grow plants on an individual basis. If one seed, only one, falls on some good soil and a plant springs up by itself, that's fine. But this is not God's best. For only one plant to grow alone and by itself is not really God's plan. **He wants a garden**.

Plants do much better when they grow together. They are much healthier. They grow faster together. And it simply looks better to the world to see a hundred beautiful flowers all clumped together than to see just one by itself growing alone in a field, as wonderful as the one plant may be. No, you see, when plants grow together, they become a *fertile, hot bed for growth*.

You will grow extremely fast and become very hardy if you grow with other plants. You will become stronger, more beautiful, and more enduring than you ever thought possible. For one reason, your roots all get tangled up below with other plant's roots. In other words, your inner life (the unseen life below the soil) becomes "knit" and entwined with the other plants. This is a wonderful experience.

The soil also stays in better condition when plants grow together. The plants all growing together can really withstand a lot of wind and heavy rains because they are so entwined and rooted together.

But what does it take for our roots to become entwined with others and for us to be knit with one another as the apostle Paul talked about in Col 2:2?

This is *the essence of life in the church*.

God's design for growth is within the context of the church. God's design for healing and restoration is in the context of the church. A lot of us know this concept but don't seem to cooperate with it very well.

One reason for our non-cooperation is that most Christians have no real example of how to live it out properly. There is also not much opportunity for true body life within the American culture. It takes tremendous courage to truly live vulnerably and transparent with others and to do it on a consistent, on-going basis.

To truly live in the light with others in deep honesty, is tremendously wonderful and sometimes tremendously painful. This is the difference between being religious and being real. We all need to learn to let down and fall apart with other brothers and sisters. Honesty with ourselves, with God, and with others on a consistent basis is what we don't want to do, but it is what we all need so desperately.

Many of us do live vulnerable with others to some degree. But even any lack of vulnerability, is not true vulnerability. To live as consistently honest and real with others, as I'm describing, to most would be unthinkable.

Resistance to Being Real

Again, the traditional religious setting fights against this. The traditional religious system does not promote this. In fact, it promotes the opposite. It promotes falseness in the disciple. The example to everyone of how to live and be in the church is lived out by the leadership in the church. The leadership provides the example of how you are to be.

How are we trained to be in traditional church? You are to be shallow and false. You are to keep your own individual space. **You should only let others in to a certain degree.** You must maintain at least some amount of distance. In a certain, sort of false humility way, you are to pretend that you have it together.

Again, our example of how to be and how to conduct ourselves is found in the leadership. Do you think, if the leadership in the traditional church setting were to really be gut-level honest with everyone about what they are REALLY like, they would be able to maintain their position as leaders? Nope. Because people's idea of what it takes to be in leadership is that you must arrive at a certain level of spirituality. People in leadership are to have a certain level of maturity. **Our idea of maturity is a lie.** There is no one that is mature (in our sense of the word). Do you want to know what a mature Christian looks like? It's someone who is a mess and knows they're a mess. It's someone who confesses their sin regularly. It's someone who comes to the light. It's someone who is so full of fault, most places would shun them, avoid them and have nothing to do with them – much less allow them to be in leadership.

In the typical church fellowship today, if you are really honest with other people about what you are really like, they will judge you, avoid you, then talk about you to others. All the while, every single person equally deals with the same weak human issues everyone else is dealing with – some form of fear, pride, lust or selfishness. Yet, if you confess these things, or others become aware of them in you, you will probably be talked about and be subtly distanced.

That's the whole problem. In most church settings there is a false role of leadership filled by men that are not completely in the light themselves. This role of leadership is then upheld and supported by people who are, for the most part, not completely in the light with one another either. If everyone would begin to be really honest, the whole thing would come crumbling down because the foundation in most fellowships is based on shallow, half hearted Christianity.

Jesus said that if you look at a woman with lust in your heart, you've committed adultery. Ok. Then let's try this:

> The pastor walks up to the podium on Sunday morning. He opens his Bible, looks at the congregations and says, "Before I preach the message today, I want to confess something to everyone. I've committed adultery about 6 times this last week. (the pastor then looks at his wife on the second pew and says, 'Sorry sweetie.') Now, for today's sermon, if everyone has their Bibles, please turn to the book of ……"

Have you ever read the book of Psalms? Do you believe that the Psalms are the written word of God? I do. Do you study the Psalms? Do you believe that we are to submit to the Psalms as the written word of

God for our lives? Yet, the Psalms were written by a man who had sex with a woman who was not his wife, and then he murdered her husband. He was even deceitful in the way he had him murdered. We are all studying and setting our lives under a book written by a murdering, adulterous, liar. By most people's standards, David is certainly not qualified to be a leader - this man after God's own heart.

Paul said he was chief of all sinners. Yet we believe he really was in a different league than the rest of us, just being falsely humble or poetic, perhaps trying to make a point, when he made such a statement.

Paul believed that statement when he said it. The man who was the chief of all sinners, wrote most of the New Testament, and we study it as God's written word.

What about Peter? He flat out denied that he knew Christ. And he did it 3 times. If there were a man among us in leadership who denied that he even knew who Christ was, and did it 3 times, we would have him removed from the pulpit. "No, sorry Peter, you cannot be a leader among us because you did this horrible thing." Yet he was an apostle and wrote 2 books of the New Testament.

The point is that the idea we have of leadership is a false rank. Because of our misinterpretation of I Tim., and what "an office" actually is, we've created, allowed, and supported a false rank to exist in the church (refer to chapter on Offices, Titles, and Gifts). It makes it *extremely* difficult for a totally honest man to live up to this false rank. Therefore, it causes men to have to be false with themselves and with others to live up to the expectations of what it means to be a leader. (The qualifications of doing overseeing work or serving in 1 Tim. do not contradict this.)

Today, to be qualified as a leader, you can have sins, but not "these certain sins." This is all falseness. The whole thing is a farce. It is all set up to cause failure. And the failure that is occurring all the time is pretended to not be failure. It is hidden and all pretended away.

Sin is more common with people then you might think. I am not saying that we have to sin. I am not saying that all people walk in sin. I am not saying that if a man is *walking* in sin, that he should be permitted to lead. Because of the power of the Spirit of God in us, we've been given the power over sin. The only way to win over sin in our lives is to live humbly and dependant on Jesus. When we are in a situation where we have to pretend that we have it together or if we are in a position that doesn't allow us to be truly just a man, it's going to promote strongholds in our lives. We are not really in the light. It is only through living humbly, broken, and in the light, that we can be victorious over sin.

Walking truly in honesty with one another in the Spirit of God, and being loved and restored from doing so, is the essence of church life.

If all you are doing is showing up to meetings (going to a meeting is only about 10% of true body life), you are not really living church life. Meetings tend to have too many people and are too infrequent to accomplish real walking in the light with one another.

We must have at least a couple of other people we are extremely current with and close with on a heart level. These are the few others that that carry us in prayer, that provide emotional support, who counsel with us, who know us deeply, and because of the blood of Jesus, love and accept us *no matter what*. These are the ones we are knit with very closely. These people will be the same gender as you are.

This very small core group you are with is not a click. Hopefully, you all are part of a larger network of believers. Some of those whom you are very closely knit with, may also be tightly knit with others as well. Overlap is essential. The group you are closely knit with is never to be closed off to others coming around and joining in at some level.

Church life is a result of multiple people who are humbly, wholeheartedly, and unreservedly loving Jesus and holding to the scriptures in their individual lives. Church life is sharing with others in vulnerability, transparency, and spontaneity. With intense accountability and prayer, church life is filled with truth and forgiveness for one another.

As you are seeking Jesus, and He is first in your life, He will lead you to be with others. Then, you get to choose.

You get to choose how deep you will go by being honest and in the light with others.

Will you receive reproof? Will you reprove others?

We must have dependence on the Lord as individuals. We must also learn to have a dependence on the Lord in one another. Therefore, we must have interdependence on one another in the Body. Will you allow yourself to need others? We need the Lord in the Body, (I Cor. 12:20-25). Although no person is to ever become our source.

When I began living New Testament body life, I was 19 years old. The older brothers mentored me, loved me, reproved me, confronted me, and encouraged me. This is how it should be for a young man in the church. I got to attend the brothers' meetings and listen to the older ones ponder and pray through multitudes of church problems. I learned quite a lot as a young man. There were many late nights with brothers confessing sins, weaknesses, and praying for one another.

In New Testament body life, there are spontaneous visits from families dropping in our home unannounced (not on a meeting night), sometimes carrying a loaf of bread with them and a bottle of wine for the Lord's supper; we often share communion together with a couple of families and end up praying the evening together. A sister might stop by our home and tell my wife that she needs to talk and pray. There are breakfasts together, weekend retreats, working together while singing praises, and looking out your window at night and seeing a fire built with saints spontaneously gathering to worship. Several of us may take a long trip together for a vacation, to visit other fellowships, or to a prison to preach the gospel, while reading and discussing scripture in the car there and back.

There are seasons when one brother might do some shepherding in my life in a particular area, and then the season comes to an end. The Lord may bring in another brother later to love me and speak into my life for a totally different area, all the while the Lord may be using me to shepherd, teach, and speak into the lives of others.

There may be frequent calls at any time of the day or in the middle of the night to pray for various needs.

There are no requirements. There is no law. The only rule is to love one another and be in the truth. Some families participate a lot. Some only participate a little. There's no possible way someone can attend every get together and every meeting. If someone did, I might question if they are meeting the needs of their natural family. There may be seasons where an individual family needs plenty of time with just themselves. Everyone supports that.

The main thing that happens to you in church life is that you are restored. You learn to trust. Not trust in people - you will really get to see plenty of weakness and mistakes in individuals. But you do learn to trust Jesus. You begin to see His hand in the church. You hear Him speak through, not only the respected ones, but through the lowly people as well. You get to know what it's really like to be loved, no matter what. You will get to humble yourself on the same issue *so many times*, that there's nothing else left to say or do, but only to receive a hug.

The church is the Lord's hands and feet. We are His body, and He will use His body to correct and love you. He will love your heart back to life. In the church, He will love you so closely and so in your face that you *will learn to trust Him.* You will grow. You will not be shaken. You will learn to weather tremendous storms.

But you will have to risk.

You will have to step out in vulnerability with your brothers and sisters. You will have to confess your apathy. And you will often bear your soul, exposing yourself to the gentle, loving, light of correction.

You will tell another person that they hurt you. Someone will inform you that you have been being selfish. You will learn to forgive at all times. And you will learn to receive forgiveness for yourself.

As you grow secure in the church's love for you, you will be able to let down more, and let down more, and more.

You will learn to love and truly honor your spouse. You will learn to raise your kids. You will become honest - because you will be required to be honest in all things.

You will live in freedom. Your prayers will change. Your life will be deepened. You will find that you have more room, more capacity, in your heart towards God. The stillness will come and you will find rest. You will journey on with your brothers and sisters, fighting the good fight of faith, and doing what you were created to do - living full throttle, and with all of your heart.

Please don't just attend meetings; Christ died for more than that. Don't use a church meeting to get your God stamp for the week, then go home, and hide in your house.

"I Don't Have Any More Time Available."

If your job or work causes you to be too busy for body life, then change jobs. What is your life about anyway - work? I highly recommend that you live off the least amount of money as possible. You should cut your spending and your monthly needs, so that you don't have to have high pressure, 60 hour a week jobs. High stress jobs steal our time and our emotional strength. A job is just a means to put food on the table and keep the lights on. Sell your house and live in a cheaper one.

If you really want the life God intended for you to live, in the context of the church, it's going to cost you. You're going to have to have some time and some heart available.

It is extremely difficult to live New Testament church life in America, and maintain the American economic standards.

If you're serious about your life in God, you're going to have to start making some different choices. It will be hard.

Your kids may not like it at first. Your spouse may have to get passed some things. But, if you want to love those around you, you must learn to give them what they need, and not necessarily what they want. Loving your family has nothing to do with giving them what they want. They need to be plugged in with healthy, growing, fervent Christians. Your family's spiritual well being and growth is far more important than getting to go to Disney World, getting to drive new cars, wearing $100 pairs of sneakers, or even living in a nice house.

You should be able to work a simple 40 hour a week job, pay your bills, and have plenty of family time available during the week, all while maintaining very close relationships within the church.

If you are trapped and caught in what seems like a hopeless situation of no time and no energy, you need to begin with prayer. God will always make a way of escape if you truly cry out to Him. When the way of escape comes, take it. However, you must be willing to sacrifice.

You should also be willing **to re-locate where you live** in order to have church life. Life is too short, and God is too good to waste your life struggling to meet the economic standards of the American lifestyle while being separated from true, New Testament, body life. You must be open to re-locating, and hooking up with some folks who are already living body life.

How To Meet

What does the church meeting look like?

It depends.

It depends on the people. It depends on the season they are in. It will depend on the culture.

In your attempts to meet together, if you predetermine how it will look, you will kill it. If you decide before hand what you are going to do, you will create two hours of dreaded torture.

The life of the Lord will dictate what the meeting looks like. To only focus on the outward of the New Testament church and try to replicate it, would spell disaster.

If your meetings are alive, then they will always change. The church meeting this year will not look like it did last year. The meeting in the Fall will probably be different than what it was in the Spring.

The church meeting in Australia will not look like the meetings in Africa. The church meetings in South Florida will not look like the meetings in India. The meetings should "fit" the people. There is no magic format.

However, there are some given foundational activities that allow us to accomplish the goals of the church meeting. The purpose of this chapter is to describe the activities that lend themselves to encountering the Lord and edifying one another.

First, let's look at what a church meeting is.

Jesus said, "For where two or three are gathered together in My name, there I am in their midst." A church meeting is anytime at least two Christians are gathered together in His name. If a brother stops by your house and invites you to run an errand with him, the ride in the car with two Christian brothers is a church meeting.

Paul tells us in a couple of different places the kinds of things we are to do when we are with others. Ephesians 5:19 tells us to *"speak to one another in psalms and hymns and spiritual songs, singing and making melody with your heart to the Lord; always giving thanks for all things in the name of our Lord Jesus Christ to God."*

Colossians 3:16, *"Let the word of Christ richly dwell within you, with all wisdom teaching and admonishing one anther with psalms and hymns and spiritual songs, singing with thankfulness in your hearts to God."*

Anytime we are with other Christians, these types of activities are wonderful to do. But there is also a different type of church meeting that Paul describes in 1 Corinthians 14.

Paul tells us in verse 26 of chapter 14, *"What is the outcome then brethren? When you assemble..."* This is not a ride in the car to the grocery store. This is when there are many gathered together to focus on the Lord. The purpose of this chapter is to give some practical examples of the kinds of things that are to go on in a general assembly meeting. This is a big subject, but tremendously simple.

Again, I hate to give any specifics here because of what the flesh will tend to do with it. The church is to be organic and spontaneous, not mechanical. It is not to be methodical. Methodology and law quench the Spirit among us. Everything we do should be from the heart and from conviction, not from habit and not from an instruction manual. However I will provide some, hopefully general, guidelines that we do see in scripture. My encouragement is to use the specific guidelines in this chapter very loosely.

We must first understand the point of coming together, then it will be easy to understand why and what we are to do. Paul tells us in I Corinthians to "let all things be done for edification." When we come together it is to love God, to worship Him, and to allow the Holy Spirit through the body to edify the body.

1 Corinthians 14:26 *"What is the outcome then, brethren? When you assemble, each one has a psalm, has a teaching, has a revelation, has a tongue, has an interpretation. Let all things be done for edification."*

This passage will be foundational for the Christian meeting, or when we all gather together.

Another very important foundation: If you look at the New Testament, prayer was a big deal. The early Christians prayed together, a lot. Paul tells us that we are to be <u>devoted</u> to prayer. The early Christians were all praying together when the Holy Spirit came at Pentecost. In Acts we read that the disciples were meeting house to house many times a week, breaking bread together and devoting themselves to prayer and to the apostles' teaching.

Prayer is a staple for the church meeting. When we gather together, we are to pray together. In fact, the attitude and posture of prayer is to permeate the entire time. Remember, we are coming together to commune with the Lord, to experience the Lord, and to edify one another.

The book of Acts tells us that the first Christians were "taking their meals together with gladness and sincerity of heart." Breaking bread together means eating together, but not just any old eating. The Christian fellowship meal is to be a time of joy, talking, and eating with thankfulness. You should not come to the fellowship meal extremely hungry. Eating and getting full is not really the point. Paul reproved the Corinthians for participating in the fellowship meal in a selfish way.

Also, there is available a cup with wine and a loaf of bread to represent the blood and body of our Lord. At some point during the meal, each believer has available to them an opportunity to sincerely partake of the cup and eat of the bread to remember what the Lord has done. One thing we are to do at the Christian meeting is to eat together and partake of the wine and bread.

Generally speaking, we can see three things we are to do when we come together.

1. We eat together with the Lord's table as the center piece.

2. We pray together.

3. We edify one another in various ways.

Let's look at what a typical church meeting might look like:

We've eaten our meal and we've had an enjoyable time of talking and visiting. We've also each sincerely taken the Lord's supper. Let's move over to the living room.

Someone may start us off with a song or two as we all begin to focus solely on the Lord. We begin by giving thanks. From our hearts, we genuinely thank Jesus for who He is and what He has done. We spend plenty of time here. No hurry. We could thank and praise Him all night for who He is and what He has done and what He is going to do! This is critical. We must be "caught up" with who Jesus is, less we risk being only earthly during our time. We give thanks for His promises. We give thanks for what He did on the cross. We give thanks for the forgiveness of sins. We give thanks for the everlasting covenant. Soon the water will become wine*** (refer to notes at end of chapter).

As we are completely focused on the goodness of God, and in love with Jesus, someone may lead out in another song. We may sing five or six songs in a row. There are more prayers of praise and more songs. As the Lord leads and as the Spirit inspires, we may pray for different needs. The Holy Spirit may put an encouraging word on someone's heart. A prophecy may come forth (prophecies may not look like a typical charismatic prophecy, they may be delivered conversationally), a scripture may be read, a teaching may be given. All of these activities are done prayerfully; in other words, if a teaching is given, we respond with prayer. Perhaps a prayer of repentance or a prayer of thankfulness for what the Lord has just reminded us of. Perhaps there may be a good long time of silence to allow the Holy Spirit time to deal with us on an individual basis.

Let all things be done for edification. Come with your heart prepared. Come ready to participate. In order to participate, you don't necessarily have to be vocal. As long as you are of faith in your heart, you can participate. In other words, participate by "amening" and agreeing with what others say. If you are quietly praying, do so with all your heart. Be listening intently for what the Lord might want to show you. Be listening to what the Lord might want to say through you to the others present. You should strongly desire to prophecy. Strongly loving those whom are in the room with you makes you a much better candidate for prophecy to come forth through you.

An important note needs to be inserted here. In whatever setting you meet in, whether it is a home, a park, a backyard, or a building – remember that it is important how you set up the chairs and the seating arrangements. This would not have to be mentioned if our perverted practices weren't so common. It is absolutely ingrained in our thinking that a church meeting must have an audience, and that the audience must be focused and facing those who are leading. In a New Testament meeting, everyone is encouraged to lead out. Therefore it is critical that we face each other. You should try to arrange the chairs in a circle or something similar. If you have a larger meeting, double stack the circle. Remember, we are family. There is no more clergy in New Testament church life. We are looking for Jesus to lead the meeting by using many people, not a man and not a small designated group of people.

The next time you and your immediate family get together for a visit in the living room, would you set the furniture up in rows and all face one family member? Of course not. So, don't do it for a church meeting either. Having all the chairs in rows, still facing a few leaders and passing a microphone around the crowd is not good enough either. First of all, try to avoid things like microphones and speaker systems. They throw us into "going to church" mode. But secondly, if you are all facing one direction, whether you pass a microphone around or not, you are saying that the people we are facing are really in charge and these are the people whom we are focused on and looking to lead the time.

When we come together outside of the traditional church, we are saying that **we are taking the responsibility to be a functioning and active member,** as opposed to being checked out and letting a staff member be active in heart or in demonstration.

It's easier to learn by doing than to read about it. Whatever you do, don't plan too much or have an agenda. Do the folks I gather with eat a meal every time we get together? No. This chapter is just here to provide some basic guidelines. God is in you. Trust Him. Let God be in charge of the meeting and trust Him to lead it. He is an orchestra conductor. He may point to the trumpets or point to the clarinet section or any member of the church to speak, to lead out, to sing, to prophecy, to encourage, to pray for someone, to ask a question to the group for all to answer, or publicly read scripture. Come to the meeting time filled with the Lord or come asking for help and prayer, but always come participating and always come expecting God to do great things in your midst.

In the heart of the New Testament instructions, we must provide an atmosphere of corporate participation in the meeting of the general assembly. This is much more than a man standing up and giving a message, then opening it up for comments from the crowd at the end.

And it is much more than the preacher asking if "every heart and mind is clear before we dismiss."

You May All Prophecy One By One

Paul uses very specific language in 1 Cor. 14: 29-32 saying:

"And let two or three prophets speak, and let the others pass judgment. But if a revelation is made to another who is seated, let the first keep silent. For you can all prophesy one by one, so that all may learn and all may be exhorted; and the spirit of prophets are subject to prophets"

This is rarely if ever practiced in the church today. And we are suffering for it. I've never seen anything close to this being practiced in traditional meetings. And in house churches it is rarely done well, if any attempt is made at all. If we can get the heart of this, it will encourage a beautiful expression of body life. Let me try to put this in very practical terms as far as the way this has been practiced with myself and those I've walked with.

Before we jump into it, keep in mind that prophetic utterances do not have to be delivered in your typical Pentecostal, charismatic flavor. You don't have to say, "thus saith the Lord" before you deliver it. A prophecy, although weighty, does not have to be religiously worded. It can simply be something like, "I feel impressed to encourage us in something…" Even that may seem religious to you. So you can say something like "I wanted to remind us of something." You don't have to say that it is from the Lord because the expectation is that everything we do and say in a meeting is from the Lord.

Ok, so we are in a meeting. A person begins to share a prophecy or an encouragement that they feel is from God. As the prophecy is being shared, someone may respectfully interrupt. How do they go about interrupting? Quietly slip your hand up and down. Hold up a finger. If it is in a larger gathering, they should stand up. The one who is speaking should be watching for and encouraging others to do that. He or she would love to be interrupted. It's part of the culture of the group. **We, *together as a group***, are trying to find what the Lord is saying to **us**. The purpose of the time is not for me to get to say what I want to say.

It's not impolite to gently interrupt, it's not disrespectful, nor does it have anything to do with someone not getting to share what they had. That's not the point of any of this. As the person gently interrupts, the speaker eagerly says, "Yes, brother – do you have more on this or something to add?" The interrupter might say, "Yes, I think we need to go back to the point you were making at first. I'm getting something on that I'd like to add."

We are looking for the Spirit in all we do. As someone shares a prophecy or a word with us, we are listening for God in it. As someone is sharing, often times they will add to the pure Word they received from God their own interpretations, insights and opinions. Some of these are helpful, some are not. Sometimes as people share and they go on and on, it takes away from what they really received from God. It is important that we help one another in this. "Brother, I think what the Lord is saying through you is this…." We should always love and want our words to be checked, interrupted, and altered by one another. It's the

Lord's way in the body. Get used to it. You should want to be interrupted.

We can all prophecy one at a time. It may need to be interrupted or slightly altered. One point someone is sharing may to be stressed because it really happens to be speaking to a lot of people in the group. This is done and accomplished corporately by more than just one person participating.

However, although it is possible for all to prophecy, only two or three prophecies should be brought forth in a meeting time. If more than that is spoken, we tend to lose and forget the earlier ones. Our capacity to retain and spiritually process a theme or a word and effectively apply it to our lives is limited by two or three per meeting. If you felt like you had something to share with the group, but three different messages have already come forth, it would be Biblical and obedient for you to let it go. If it is the Lord, He will bring it back around at a later time. This is not about us getting to share or speak. It's about us hearing what the Lord is saying to us. If someone interrupts you before you get to your point, let it go. If what you had was the Lord, He will bring it back around or bring it up in you at a later time. ***We must learn to trust the Lord in the Body***.

Let's look at the "let the others pass judgment" part of the text. After a prophecy, message, or encouragement is shared, we should tend to be silent. We need to take it in. We need to think about it. We need to pray. It's weighty when someone shares something in the church meeting. No matter who it is that shared it. Is God speaking to us? If He is, we'd better humble ourselves, shut up, and do what He says. If there is not a witness in the Spirit or if what has been shared is not Biblical, it needs to be checked. The older brothers need to say something. It doesn't need to be rejected in a cutting way. It doesn't need to be rejected at all up front, unless it is clearly unscriptural. If what was shared seems good to the group, then one of two responses would be good: either nothing can be said, or a hearty "Amen" can be given. If it is perceived as not being good, from God, Biblical, or edifying, an older brother needs to say something like, "this last message or prophecy needs some more prayer and consideration. We as a group need to wait on the Lord concerning this issue." Or something like that. Then, it would be good for the brother who shared it to have some time with others to talk about and pray together. The person who delivered the word may come to the conclusion that it was not the Lord at all. It would be good for them to simply tell everyone else at the next get together, that "I think I missed it."

I have been in meetings when a brother has shared something, and an older brother (elder) just flat out said, "I'm sorry brother, that's not the Lord." There was an atmosphere at that time in our group for that kind of thing. The older brother who said that to the one who brought the prophecy also had a relationship with him that could support that type of thing. They both had a tremendous amount of love and respect for one another and it was delivered in kindness. The brother whose prophecy was rejected, didn't skip a beat. He responded thankfully and was not hurt at all. He continued to participate in the meeting. I've also been checked like this myself on a few different occasions. It really doesn't bother me, I like it.

We really are not very far along, if as a group, we can't have this type of dynamic among us. The Christian life is a high calling. We must die to everything of ourselves. Real New Testament church life will provide tremendous opportunities for growth.

The heart of this whole 1 Cor. 14 passage should permeate our meeting times. If in a meeting, a brother stands up and delivers a lengthy teaching, he should welcome others to interrupt and add to the message. He might get to only share a portion of what he wanted to share. He should let it go. If he wants to teach and not be interrupted, which is very appropriate at times, then he should call for a special meeting of the church. This is a special meeting to hear a message or a teaching only. This is good and should be done often. However *it is not to be confused with the regular meeting of the church, the general assembly or the default meeting we are to be having described in*

1 Corinthians 14.

Fear is what drives many of those in leadership to not have open, 1 Cor. 14 meetings. They are afraid of giving too much liberty to the people in the meeting. They do not trust the Lord in the body. They do not trust the New Testament pattern and examples. They feel as though people are not spiritually mature enough to handle such a meeting. *They are actually the ones who are not being spiritually mature.*

Control and legislation are never the answers for fear. We must learn to trust, let go, and follow the Lord and the scriptures. *There will be problems!* It will be messy at times. People will mess up the meeting. People will speak out of turn. People will share things that are not good, are bad, and things that are not scriptural. This will all happen especially at first when people are learning. These things must be addressed and people must be talked to. You must provide training and teaching (refer to Beach Head and Well Digging chapter).

People need to learn by doing. **Provide an atmosphere of safety for people to function, make mistakes, and for it to be OK.** This is how we will learn to be a functioning, powerful, active, and participating church. If we are really interested in people growing and learning, then set them free to function and make mistakes. Some of the best and most valuable character building issues of growth come from us relating to one another in our mistakes and in our gifts. Learn how to do it together. Growth does not come by us lecturing people and giving them teachings and seminars year after year after year! We've tried that and look where it has gotten us. People learn and grow by having an atmosphere that not only sincerely welcomes and encourages them to participate in their gifts, **but an atmosphere and a setting that actually needs and depends on all members to bring what they have and deliver it during every meeting.**

It must be understood that the descriptions and explanations that Paul gives in 1 Corinthians 14 is for a typical church meeting and a general assembly. There may be other meetings for different purposes and we see evidence of these in the New Testament. There may be a meeting in which the sole purpose is to hear someone give a teaching. There may be a meeting in which the sole purpose is to only pray together. There may be a meeting in which the only purpose is to discuss some particular issue. These special meetings are not what Paul is describing in I Cor. 14.

***[In the Christian experience, there seems to be a *breaking through* that can occur. I don't fully understand it. It is not only true for a group meeting, but

---

101

also for our personal lives as well. As individuals or corporately, we can pray, talk to the Lord, think about Him, sing, whatever, and all of that is necessary....but if we stay in that place long enough, if we focus on Jesus long enough, if we finally let go in our hearts to real trust, if we still ourselves in our soul and become completely caught up with Him, something happens. I call it breaking through or the "water becoming wine." I'm not very sure on the theology of this, but I am sure of the experience - both individually and corporately. It is always wonderful to break through corporately. When this happens, the Spirit of the Living God seemingly physically fills the room. Many call it experiencing God's presence. Sometimes it is more pronounced than other times. It usually occurs after there has been much worship and singing and complete focus on the Lord and Him alone. This is usually when the Lord is very powerfully manifested among us (He inhabits the praises of His people). I believe that worship and prayer are two of the most pure activities we can do, that doesn't tend to quench the Spirit as often as some form of talking can. It must be noted that our **goal** is never to have an experience. Although having an experience is wonderful if that is what happens. Our goal is to love Jesus, to know Him, and to love and edify one another. We are not to manipulate, try to reproduce, or create an effect.]

How *Not* To Meet

Plenty of house churches and untraditional gatherings just fizzle out. Why? I think primarily because of the information in this chapter.

We want freedom and liberty in our meeting times, but there are some terrible mistakes we can make when coming together that bring death. We want life among us. We want to bless the Lord and encounter Him.

Here is what NOT to do:

Don't debate scripture and theology.

There are two types of flesh. There is truth-oriented flesh and experience-oriented flesh. I call it flesh because Jesus said we must worship in Spirit **and** in truth. If you have one without the other, you are fleshly. Some people don't like the activities of singing, worship, and prayer very much. They judge it as trying to have an experience or trying to have some sort of a feeling. They would prefer to hear teaching or discuss doctrine. These people are usually not opposed to singing a few songs, but if you spend too much time worshiping in song or too much time in prayer, they get very fidgety.

The capacity of a group or an individual to worship and pray is a strong indicator of the real depth you have with Christ. Discussing doctrine can have tremendous life in it, as long as it's not done in an argumentative way. Also, having sound doctrine, teaching, and the ability to discuss these in a <u>proper manner</u> and at <u>the proper time</u> are also strong indicators of the real depth you have with Christ. We must have plenty of worship and prayer, but also plenty of discussion and teaching of truth.

Again, the flesh tends to prefer one or the other. We tend to prefer either the experience of the Spirit, or learning about or talking about the truth. We must beware of discussing the truth only. Usually, this activity doesn't require much vulnerability of heart. If someone can't really worship the Lord for any length of time and they get restless during this type of activity, they more than likely tend to be cranial and on the conceptual side of things only. These brothers and sisters need to learn to enjoy the Lord more in stillness and quietness. They must learn to be caught up with the Lord in experience. Experiencing the Spirit of Jesus is both vital and Biblical. On the other hand, those who prefer to experience only and avoid doctrine, working things out, and dealing with truth are in error as well. These must learn to deal with discrepancies and be willing to hash out things with others. Lord, help us all!

Concerning debating scripture, doctrine, and theology: <u>I am not saying there is not a time and a place for this.</u> During the general meeting of the church is not the time for debate. Why? It's not a time for debate because 1st Corinthians Chapter 14 never comes close to anything like this. It seems so many people love to do it and consider it an essential part of the church meeting. I would say that a large majority of Christians think this activity is what fellowship is all about. These people would probably enjoy discussing politics as well. It's as though some aren't sure what else to do when they come together. Paul warns us of "having a morbid interest in controversy," (I Tim.6:3). Debate, apologetics, and intellectual jousting typically have no life in them, although some form of this may need to be done at certain times.

First of all, the ladies and the children should not have to listen to men correcting one another and entering into debate. The women are fragile (or at least they should be) and can easily be shaken or tempted with fear.

It is critical that we keep short accounts with one another. If there is a difference in doctrine with someone else, watch your heart very carefully because differences can cause a subtle division in the heart. If not dealt with, over time it will manifest itself and cause damage. It needs to be dealt with if there are any feelings of separation.

If in a meeting a brother shares a doctrine or teaching and someone disagrees, let the disagreeing man pull aside the brother with the doctrine in question and talk through it. If in the meeting with everyone present, someone wants to add to what someone said that's fine. Providing a gentle flip side to the coin can be helpful. But, don't start going "back and forth" and arguing with one another in the general church meeting! If you can tell that you will need to really hash it out, do it in private and possibly with a couple of additional brothers for help and support.

If some of the men are taking issue with one another (disagreeing), it is best that they set up a separate time with just men present, and work things out. The men may have to go at it intensely, and that's just fine - as long as it's done in love, with patience, and the brothers are genuinely listening for God and wanting to truly hear and learn from one another (refer to the chapter "Church Government"). In the past, I've personally set days at a time aside to do this sort of thing with the brothers. There should be no mistake made however that this activity of working out differences, debating theology or beliefs is sometimes a necessary WORK, but it is not typically extremely enjoyable. If this activity is your primary idea of what body life is all about, then your repentance is due.

The scripture of "as iron sharpens iron, so one man sharpens another," has been overused and also wrongly used. Sometimes, in order to provide justification to men for not being worshipful and prayerful, as they are around each other. The "iron" in that scripture does not allow us to be rough, hard hearted, or challenging (as in fighting).

Although it is excellent in our meeting times to read scripture, give in depth teachings, share beliefs and convictions, and talk about what the Lord has been doing in our lives, if you are spending the majority of your time in your meetings **debating** theology or controversial issues, it's going to get old quickly. The number of people attending will drop off, and eventually you will fizzle out, or you will attract a church of fighters and debaters. Debate and intellectual only conversation is easy to do. It requires no discipline, no heart, no humility, and no selflessness. In a gathering, be slow to speak. You shouldn't say everything that pops into your head. Wait on God in the church meetings. It is only with humility that we can encounter the living God and not offend or quench Him.

Don't sit around and just visit.

Visiting and chewing the fat is great to do during a meal time. But when it's time to sit together and focus on the Lord, do just that. The church meeting is not to be spent visiting and chatting about the repairs you made on your car or the latest sale at the shopping mall. Do what it takes to change the atmosphere in the room. Don't wait for someone else to do it. Just say the words, "I have a song I would like for us to sing", then sing it together. Say, "I have a scripture I'd like to read to us." Those types of activities will change the focus in the room towards the Lord.

Don't expect or just rely on others to bring something.

If you are wanting to leave the traditional church setting and begin to meet in New Testament ways, what you are really saying is something like this:

"I don't need a paid staff member to be the only one that participates and functions in the meetings. We don't want a man to lead the meetings, but we want the Holy Spirit to lead the meetings. The Spirit of God might call on me to share something. I am ready to begin to take more responsibility in my life with God. I don't want to just soak up and be fed, I want to participate, contribute, and I am willing to give to others what I have from my own relationship with God."

It's time to stop looking to others to take initiative. Lead out with what you have. YOU DO HAVE SOMETHING. It doesn't matter where you are spiritually. It may be that all you have on a particular night is a need. You can always ask for prayer. If you have no need, then you just discovered your first need! Be a participator. Bring whatever you have. You can always read a psalm, share what the Lord has been teaching you, ask for a particular song to be sung, pray a prayer, ask for others to pray for you, or bring a teaching. Don't depend on and look to others to carry the meeting. Amen? OK.

Don't try to imitate a traditional, Sunday morning, 10:45 a.m. meeting in a home.

Some are looking to start or participate in a home church in order to replace their former traditional church setting. To just hold "services" in your home instead of sitting on the pew is really missing the heart of the Lord and the entire purpose of our gathering together. You might as well go to a traditional service where they do a better job holding that kind of meeting than anything you could reproduce in a home. If you haven't had the revelation of not having to have pews, a pulpit, dress up for meetings, meet at 10:45 a.m., pass a plate to tithe in, etc. then you need to re-read the New Testament – you'll find none of that in the scripture. You'll only find it in the heart of those who believe all that is holy and "officially God." A good litmus test is to see if you feel guilty for not meeting on Sunday mornings.

The word "service" is never used in the New Testament as reference to a meeting of the church. The word is a tradition of men that has a particular religious package associated with it. A "real service," in most people's opinion, has certain things along with it – none of which are Biblical and all of which are detrimental to body life. What would happen in the middle of the next church service on Sunday morning during the preacher's sermon if someone stood up and said, "The anointing has passed to me, I feel I have a prophecy to share, please be seated" (I Cor. 14)? Would the pastor humbly say, "Amen, you go ahead and share brother." No he wouldn't. This is because the pastor is the designated teacher on Sunday morning. The Biblical role of a shepherd looks nothing like the modern day pastor, and the Sunday morning meeting time looks nothing like I Cor. 14.

Don't have a bulletin, much of a plan or any certain agenda.

Let the Lord Jesus be the head of the body, not your meeting agenda. The time should flow and be spontaneous. Enjoy the Lord. Don't try to accomplish certain things on a list. Be very careful of being formal, and be very careful of not being prayerful.

Don't be afraid of silence.

It's a wonderful thing to sit in silence together and pray, listen to God, and just be still before Him. It is better to be silent and be "of faith," than to rattle off a song or a scripture because the silence was awkward to your flesh. Get over it. There may be very long periods of silence in the meeting of the church. That's a good thing. It's been frowned upon in the traditional services because of the show and production mentality. This leads to shallowness. Good long periods of silence can be refreshing and a good time of personal and corporate faith and prayer.

When having a group conversation, don't simply add things to the conversation because you can.

If you all as a group are teaching and encouraging one another, listen to God for what you should add. Listen and be prayerful as to what and when you should add something. Remember; let all things be done for edification. It is **the Spirit** that edifies and gives life, not your brain power. JUST BECAUSE YOU HAVE AN INSIGHT DOESN'T MEAN IT'S GOD. Neat little comments you can share or add that seem to fit right in with what's being shared are not necessarily the Lord. DON'T TALK TOO LONG and TAKE OVER THE MEETING! If you have a very long teaching that you know ahead of time will be extensive, call for a separate meeting over at your own house to do a teaching for everyone. The general meeting of the church is - for the church to all participate.

Be careful of publicly praying too long as an individual. The scripture warns us of that. Beware of long stories and comments that are really just edifying your own self. House church can be a platform for people who love to hear themselves talk. These men need to be corrected very gently (the first time) in private. It is sometimes difficult to tell what is not good and edifying and what is good to share. Two Christians can share just as long (time wise) and one is being selfish and the other is truly giving. This really gets into subtle dynamics, and you'll definitely have to trust the Lord for all this kind of discernment, but generally speaking, you can usually tell if you are being built up and fed by the message or if you're being used and held captive so someone can speak.

Don't be meeting centered.

This is critical, and really a major point. If all you are doing is having meetings, you are really missing it all. Meetings, although very important, are a small part of church life. Life is to be lived together. You should be getting together with other saints throughout the week. You can participate together with activities such as barbeques, cookouts, trips to the park, working together on each others houses, camping, vacations with other families, evangelism events, and eating supper together often during the week. If all you want is to attend a meeting once a week in a home, you are not living church life at all. The meeting time should be an expression of your week together. Your week together should be an expression of the meeting time as well. The New Testament church met many times a week from house to house, and not because they had to, but because they wanted to. When Christ becomes your whole life and your whole world, instead of part of your life, you'll want to have church life 24/7.

Don't become naval gazers.

As the church, we should be primarily focused outward, not inward. Sure, we MUST keep our home base healthy. We must deal with situations in the group, we must love one another and speak the truth in love to one another, but a sure way to kill a group is to focus only on yourselves.

Evangelistic events, giving in various ways to your neighborhood, reaching out to the lost in some capacity, feeding the poor, visiting nursing homes and orphans, helping the widows – all of these should have a real primary focus. We should not be extremely focused on our group, although there may be seasons of this to get "out of the red ink." You'll find that as you get more outwardly focused, the inner problems will become lessoned. Sometimes, the best way to find healing for yourself is to go love someone else.

Church Government

When we talk about church government, we are speaking of church leadership. Who is calling the shots? Who is qualified? Why are they qualified? What kinds of decisions need to be made?

The New Testament speaks of the leadership in the church by using the words *elders or overseers*. Keep in mind that the body of elders were given to a church in a city, not a small group within the city. This is huge and must be understood. Refer to the chapter "One church in a city." We will cover the difficulties this has caused later during this chapter.

The word presbytery comes from the Greek word presbuteros, which means *elder*. Leadership by elders, plural, is found throughout the scripture.

When God sent Moses to deliver the Israelites from the Egyptians, Moses was told to "gather the *elders* of Israel together and say to them, 'The Lord God of your fathers, the God of Abraham, of Isaac, and of Jacob, appeared unto me ....'" (Exodus 3:16)

In the Old Testament, elders provided leadership and were the representatives of the people, (Deut. 21:19; Exodus 24:1; Num. 11:16; Lev. 4:15).

Elders were present in the time of the judges (1 Sam. 16:4), the period of the kings (1 Sam. 16:4; 2 Kings 19:2), and the time of captivity (Ezek. 8:1; 14:1; 20:12). Elders provided leadership in the rebuilding of the temple after the return from captivity (Ezra 5:5, 9; 6:78, 14). Information on Jewish history during the intertestamental period also bears witness to the leadership of elders in the synagogues.

When Jesus came in the New Testament, we also see references to the elders, rulers, and rulers of the synagogue(Matt. 15:2; Mark 7:3; John 3:1; 7:26, 48; Mark 5:22; Luke 8:41; cf. Acts 18:8,17).

It is important to realize that there was a continuity of government within the church in both the Old and New Testaments. The apostles did not create something radically new; they built upon what was already established in the Old Testament. When the apostles talked about church offices, the hearers recognized much of the governmental framework which was already in place. Therefore, leadership by elders is not only a New Testament church government; it is *Biblical* church government.

The modern day idea of one man calling the shots for a group is not Biblical, nor does it work. Having a pastor with a board of deacons really telling him what to do behind the scenes is also another sick tradition of men.

In the New Testament church, there was only one church in a city and the elders were recognized publicly by a true apostle. The elders operated and functioned for the church in one locality or city. We do not have that basic framework to build from today. I can literally count on one hand the people I've met, who I believe, understand and have a true depth of revelation that on a practical level that ***only geography should divide the church***. As a result of our current practice, we have multiple pockets of believers meeting in separate groups within the same locality. It's not a problem that there are many meetings and gatherings in a city. The early church had the same practice. But all the gatherings had their identity in the one group that they all belonged to, the church in the whole city. The fact remains that without the proper understanding that there is only one church in a city, we are only left with multiple "churches" each having their own autonomous authority. The elders or leadership in one assembly do not have any authority in a different assembly, even if they are located within blocks of one another.

Because we continue to practice division in the church and do not adhere to one church in any given locale, the basic New Testament way of a group of elders being given to a city or locality of believers is not available – unless the whole town takes down their signs, abandons the names of their "churches" and all come together under one name (such as the church at Corinth, the church at Philippi, the church in Denver, the church in Franklin).

Although we have quite a mess today, the very heart of the leadership pattern does not have to be lost. As we all meet together in whatever form of fellowship we are in, the heart of the New Testament example is that it only makes sense that the older guys who have been around for awhile would be heavily involved in decisions. These days, in a typical fellowship, the elders would not be appointed by an apostle (a sent out one), but the older men who are in the Lord and have the overseeing qualifications and abilities should function as such.

Does the fact of plural eldership mean that **any** older man should be in on making decisions for the church? What about the rest of us who are not older? We will answer these questions as the chapter unfolds.

An extremely important observation should be noticed at this point. Although in the New Testament we do see a group of elders being very involved in decision making, we also see plenty of examples of ***the whole assembly making decisions together and bringing closure on issues***.

Basically, the idea is that decision making or change in direction for a group should be done in a plural setting. I see a consistent thread in scripture that would look something like the following in a modern setting:

Brothers meeting, Saturday morning 9:00 AM

Who is there?

The older men who have been around a while are there. We may call them the brothers who tend to lead out a lot. If there are brothers in our midst who are very involved or who care deeply about church matters, then they should be there.

Does that include every brother? No. Some of the guys that we are meeting with may not be as involved. That is not a bad thing at all. I would say that in a larger size group, that many brothers would be of the mindset to simply work at their job, love their family, love the brethren, have a family over for a meal during the week, attend the meetings of the church and that's about it. For many brothers, they will be able to adequately function in their gifts of serving and loving others and not ever feel the need to be in on decision making meetings for the church. If everyone decided that we needed to meet on Tuesdays instead of Mondays or that we should be doing more evangelism on Saturday mornings is not really a big concern of theirs. They are happy and quite content to trustingly go with the flow.

Back to the Saturday morning meeting: Is anyone excluded from this meeting? No. It is not a closed meeting. If anyone wants to come, let them come. One brother may want his fourteen year old son present to sit in and listen for training purposes. That's fine.

What about ladies? Anyone who has read the New Testament is aware of 1 Cor.11 that describes the authority structure in that that the husband is the head of the wife and that Christ is the head of the man. If a lady has valuable input or concerns, it would be proper for her to discuss it with her husband. If he felt it was the Lord speaking, he could make it his own and then bring it up to the brothers. I do not think it is profitable for ladies to be put in a position to have to discuss heavy issues, or have a "back and forth" discussion with other men. Also, if another man shares an erroneous idea concerning direction for the church, another man way want to lovingly "crush" his idea. Sometimes it may be sharp. A man should not have to do this with a woman. It is not proper for a man to enter into debate with a lady.

What goes on during this meeting?

Prayer takes place. There is plenty of worship. There are discussions of church matters. There is more prayer. There are discussions of overview, the big picture, the direction the group is going, and issues of vision. Then, there is more prayer. How are the meetings going? What should be changed? What is good? What should we keep? What should we stop doing and why? Various needs in the body are presented and discussed. Brothers or sisters who may need to be pursued are mentioned. More prayer takes place. Current difficulties or anything that needs to be worked out may also be addressed. If at all possible, none of this should be done in an argumentative way. The time should be saturated with prayer. If a man has a problem with another brother, he should go to him in private if at all possible. Then, there should be some more prayer.

I guess you get where I'm at on corporate prayer. Talking in a group tempts people. Not that it doesn't need to be done, but talking about issues or difficulties can be a temptation to pick up an offense, to feel like someone has corrected you, or that someone spoke "down to you." Then, you are tempted to retaliate and correct the brother who corrected you because you were hurt or offended.

I've been in countless meetings discussing issues and working through things in the church. These meetings are a real test to see what you're made of. Staying humble and truly listening to one another can be a real trial. To feel accused or attacked by an individual or even a whole group and to just sit there and take it or to truly respond in peace and not out of a reaction will really test your bottom line. Sometimes we will work through some real heavy and sensitive issues and stay totally at peace as a group. Many times we truly find the Lord's heart on the issue, and it turns out extremely well. Sometimes we will start out fleshly and irritated and end that way as well.

The point is that you will do much better as a group as these times are interrupted often with prayer. Be slow to speak, prepare your heart and stay committed and devoted to one another - no matter what.

As issues are discussed, there is to be a humble and natural tendency to defer to the older men, to the ones with spiritual authority, and to the group as a whole. There should be a strong climate in the room of wanting to really hear one another. We should regard each input as very important. And more than anything, we should want to defer and "go with" the other brother's opinion if we can. We should consider each opinion heavily, because it could actually be God speaking to us.

Then What?

As the brothers come to some closure on issues or topics, it would be Biblical to throw it out to the rest of the church in the next meeting time.

Let's look at a few examples of when and how decisions were made plural in the early church.

Acts 6:5 – *"But the statement found approval with the whole congregation."*

This is referring to the incident when the apostles did not want to take time to serve tables but wanted to fully spend their time speaking and preaching. They summoned the congregation and told them what they wanted to do which was for some of the other disciples to serve the tables. Why does it say that the statement found approval with the whole congregation? Because it's important that it did find approval. If the church had a problem with it, there would be disharmony and dissension. It was good that the apostles communicated because it gave opportunity for everyone to join in with the new idea and go with the flow. There was no place for disjointedness or men doing their own thing without communicating. Even the apostles saw fit to communicate with the others what they were thinking. This communication was not with the purpose of having a vote. Throwing it open to everyone is not for the sole purpose to see if someone disapproves, but only because it's common sense. How strange it would be for a man to lead out with something that involved and affected everyone without saying something first to everyone. The apostles with great honesty and frankness even told them the purpose and reason for their plan. They didn't want to spend time serving tables. They said it and didn't protect anyone from the truth. Everyone joined in and they were all in it together. The apostles did not avoid communicating as to head off a possible confrontation or discrepancy. They just said what they were planning and was as simple as that.

More Examples of the Group Being Involved

Acts 1:15-26.

This is when Peter *"stood up in the midst of the brethren (a gathering of about 120 persons were there together) and said…..."* Basically, we need to choose someone to fill the place of Judas. The point is that he said what he thought to a whole lot of people. There is safety and freedom in the body. Someone would have checked him if he was off.

Often in the book of Acts, they were ALL TOGETHER in one place, then a man stood up and said what he thought should happen, then they ALL DID IT TOGETHER. Everyone had the opportunity to be a part of the plan, the purpose, and the heart behind it, and the execution of it. I'm sure there were many there among the 120 who had no opinion of the matter. That is fine and to be expected. **They did not all vote.** But they all did it together.

I hope you read Acts chapter 15 for yourself. You'll see that they were not afraid to talk, speak and work things out together. Men stood up and said things. They great and the small heard it all. It is pretty clear that not everyone was part of the decision making process. That's not the point. The point is that everyone **was included to hear, support, and have opportunity to join in.** The early church did not avoid messes.

Ch 15 V 34 *"But it seemed good to Silas to remain there"*. Does this contradict? No way. A man can always do what he wants independently of everyone else and it is not necessarily sin. And ultimately we know that the head of every man is Christ. But when the body is present and available, why would we want to do things independently? When we **avoid, protect, and do not want to** throw things out to the body, something is off. There is no need for decision making to rest with an individual or even a group of limited individuals when true body life is present.

I see an ongoing, open men's meeting as being vital to healthy church government. The brothers should move together, giving preference to the older ones as much as possible.

Those who have the "rule" over you?

These couple of verses, which often have been misinterpreted concerning church government, have giving place to men controlling others.

1 Tim. 5:17 *"Let the elders that rule well be counted worthy of double honor, especially they who labor in the word and doctrine.*

In Hebrews 13:17 *"Obey them that have the rule over you, and submit yourselves: for they watch for your souls, as they that must give account, that they may do it with joy, and not with grief: for that is unprofitable for you.*

The word "rule" here is the Greek word proistemi, which means "to set or place before, to set over, to be over, to superintend, preside over to be a protector or guardian, to give aid, to care for, give attention."

To be subject to an older brother is to realize that he has some years on you in the Lord. It simply means that it would be very beneficial to listen to the older guys and to those with more experience. Why? Because they probably know more than you do. The whole idea we have created of leaders making sure the non-leaders submit is not God's way. No one is to make anyone submit. Nowhere does it say for husbands to **require** the wives to submit. They should do it on their own because it is fitting. Even unbelievers know that those who have gone before them and are older, typically know more, have wisdom, and should be listened to. This is not an authority structure Peter is setting up here. Peter is just saying it would be unprofitable for the younger guys to not listen to the older wiser brothers. "Who have the rule over you," – those who are teaching you, have gone before you, are protecting or guarding over your life in God. **This is not a legal binding authority structure.** There may be an older brother who is not spiritually mature who God has not used to teach you anything. Those who are more mature than you and actually make it a practice to help you in your life – don't resist them.

The person "who has the rule over you" can change. Remember, the only true authority is the Word of God. As different people in the Body have the Word of God for your life or your particular situation, then they have the rule over you. But, it is really the Word of God that has the rule over you. God can use someone in your life for a while, then they could go off the deep end, this doesn't mean you should submit to their ideas if they go off in error. The Lord may use a particular person to speak His Word to you for a season, then He may use someone else. We should listen to those who are having the rule over us.

Those who have the rule over us, is a spiritual dynamic. It can change for different seasons, for different areas, and for different needs. One brother may have the rule over you in the area of finances. A different brother may have the rule over you in the area of eating right. It is more that you recognize their wisdom or authority in these areas and you actually give them the rule over you voluntarily, as the Lord leads you to do so.

It can also happen that someone who is not older than you can have the rule over you. Many times, your peers and those who are younger in the Lord than you will have the word of the Lord for your life. If you are listening for God in one another, you will hear others speak into your life, no matter their age or status. Remember that God uses the foolish things to shame the wise. He often reveals His wisdom to babes and not the wise and intelligent. Jesus came into Jerusalem riding on a donkey. That's His style. He doesn't usually come to you in the ways you may typically expect, because He is speaking to the humble and to those who are truly seeking. Don't miss Him because of the package the message is in.

How beautiful it is when an older brother receives instruction from a younger one. It is the Word of God that has the authority, not men or the vessel. It is very possible for a younger man to have the rule over you because God has given him wisdom into your particular situation or weakness.

Now, keep in mind that the King James translates 1 Peter 5:5 in saying *You younger men, likewise, be subject to your elders; and all of you, clothe yourselves with humility* **toward one another**, *for God is opposed to the proud, but gives grace to the humble.*

In the above passage we see that we are to all to have humility toward one to another. Peter is saying that the younger folks should listen to the older folks that have been teaching them and speaking into their lives. But also that everyone should have humility and be subject to one another. We should all listen to God in one another!

Ephesians 5:19-21 says, "*...speaking to one another in psalms and hymns and spiritual songs, singing and making melody with your heart to the Lord; always giving thanks for all things in the name of our Lord Jesus Christ to God, even the Father; and be subject to one another in the fear of Christ.*"

This is a beautiful verse, and one of my favorites in the New Testament. As Paul is telling us the kinds of things we should be doing in everyday body life, he also tells us that we should be **mutually subject (submitted) to one another.**

Since Paul was on the subject of submission, in the very next verse in Ephesians 5:22, Paul gives us a very different directive concerning submission. Paul tells us*, "Wives, be subject to your own husbands, as to the Lord."* This "as to the Lord" part is a real big deal. It does not mean "because the Lord said to." It means that the wives are to receive instruction and leading from their husband as if it was the Lord Himself leading. I will not get into the topic of husbands and wives here, it is not my point. There is a clear explanation of this in a number of passages. The point is that Paul makes a distinction between the type of submission wives have with husbands, as opposed to the mutual submission that we are all to have with one another. Paul makes an extreme point when he describes a wife submitting to her husband as "unto the Lord." He does not use this type of language anywhere else in relating to each other. **Mutual submission concerning brothers is not the same submission as wives relating to husbands.**

As a side note, I must insert that there is a verse in the Old Testament (Isaiah 9:6) that speaks of the Messiah saying "the government will be on His shoulders." I've personally observed saints use this verse to say that we should **not** have to be concerned with church government because the Lord is in charge of things like that. The word government in this verse simply means "dominion" or "rule." The purpose of the verse is to describe and testify of who Christ is in His power and sovereignty. It is stating that He will have dominion. It is in no way excusing us from having to deal with government among us. This verse is not to be used to justify the practice of ignoring situations and to not deal with anything openly and honestly.

Establishing a Beach Head of Intimacy and Vulnerability in the Spirit

It has been said that if you desire community, you will destroy community. But if you desire to love the brethren, you will build up and establish community.

Every group has a culture about it. There are ways that we tend to be. We tend to have a certain heart posture as a group. There is certain vocabulary that each group tends to use.

Whatever is the **easiest** and the most natural for us to step into reveals the culture of the group. The conversations that are easiest for us to have indicate the culture of the group. The activities that are easiest for us to do together are an indicator of the culture of the group. On the contrary, the conversations and activities which tend to be more difficult for us to have and do, also indicate what the culture is not.

The culture or climate of any group is dictated by the foundation that it has. A group of people may know and believe that their sins are forgiven and that Jesus is the Christ, and therefore may be Christians. But how easy is it for that group to pray together? How easy is it for the group to share and talk together in an intimate and vulnerable way? Are they being knit together on a heart level?

Or, on the other hand, is it easier for us as a group to talk about fishing? Is it easier for us to just go shopping together and hang out? Is it easier for us to just talk about theology? Is it easier for us to engage in intellectual and philosophical topics? If you were riding in the car with another person of your group, would it be awkward to pray together about intimate things?

Occasionally, we may know how to do things like help someone move their furniture. We know how to serve one another with things like mowing their grass, letting them borrow our car, or visiting someone in the hospital when they're sick. But as a culture we are totally unfamiliar with how to meet one another in a deep way and on a daily basis. Things like engaging one another in tenderness through conversation. We tend to not be very good at being sensitive to one another's needs by listening to the Spirit's promptings for one another - even when we are not with one another. We are unfamiliar with and typically have little desire to want to minister to the Lord corporately through prayer (Acts 13:2).

As a culture, we are very familiar with the outward and the shallow. But we don't know much at all about the inward and about the nuisances of the heart. We don't know about it for ourselves, let alone for others or in a group setting. Phrases like "being transparent', "vulnerability," "intimacy", "the heart" – can all be elusive. The culture of the West has infected the church. We've not had much example. We've not been taught. Yet we all crave the very things we don't know much about.

In military terms, when an army wants to take over another country that is not their own, they can establish what is called a **beach head.** The invading army has to take a very small, but fortified area of territory, usually on the beach of the country being invaded. Once the invading army has landed on the beach and fortified the area, they can slowly advance and take over the country. A beach head is for taking new territory. It must be strong and it must advance slowly, otherwise it will be scattered.

In the same way, if a group of Christians are wanting to take new territory, specifically unfamiliar territory, a beach head must be established. A beach head is the easiest and most effective way of taking new ground and changing the culture of a group. If you just try to "all start praying together more" – it will be hard to make such a change.

Let's take one example. We will use this example in this chapter because this is very common. Suppose we have a group of believers for whom it happens to be very easy for them to just hang out together, but there really isn't much vulnerability or things of the Spirit going on. They long for more intimacy with God and with one another, but aren't sure exactly how to get there. Talking more about vulnerability won't help. Doing more teaching on it won't really help. Reading a book about it won't do much either. You need to do it. But you need to do it in a way that brings life and in a way that builds and takes territory in the spirit realm.

Well Digging Groups Establish A Beach Head in the Spirit

If you have multiple families together, to establish a beach head for any area you must start very small. This very small group will be like digging a well. It is hard to dig a well. You must take dirt and soil out of the ground in order for water to fill it. This is a picture in the Spirit. This very small group will be doing a very hard work of going against the grain. They will be going against the natural culture of what they are used to. They will be removing natural things (soil and dirt) and allowing the water of the life of God fill the new capacity they have forged out.

Let's start with two or the most, three people. If you want to establish a beach head of intimacy in the Spirit, these two or three need to learn how to **minister to the Lord in prayer**.

When most people think of praying together, they think of praying through a list of needs. Although the well digging group may ask God for needs, this is not the primary purpose of the group or for the time they've set aside. You must learn to see Jesus. Give thanks. Enjoy who He is. Worship Him together in song (without a CD player). Read a short prayerful verse in scripture, then rejoice and give thanks to God in prayer again. Be caught up together with the goodness and character of God. Be filled with the Spirit – together. Learn the discipline of staying in this place for a long time. It will go against everything in your flesh. Everything of flesh must die off during this time.

This is all very hard for most people to do, and their capacity for such an activity is usually very small. Most want to hurry up and start praying for various needs. As your mind thinks of various needs you could pray for, let them go, especially early on in the session. If it was the Holy Spirit leading you to pray for such a need, He will give it back to you later in the time to pray for it. Learn to be still. Quiet your souls corporately. Learn to be comfortable together in silence as you are waiting on the Lord and still being full of faith.

As this small group is caught up with Jesus and Jesus alone, then trust the Holy Spirit to lead your prayers. He will probably lead you to confess faults and sins while in prayer, with the others present. I am reminded of a song that goes like this:

"Nothing hidden, no reason to be ashamed.

Nothing hidden, no reason to be ashamed.

Exposed to your loving eyes.

No reason for words to join us.

We just are together for all time.

We just are together for all time.

With nothing hidden, no reason to be ashamed."

Learn to have a very peaceful, intimate, vulnerable time in the Holy Spirit and with one another.

Now here is a real key. Add people to your well digging group very slowly. Start with two or three, but then add one brother or sister at a time and over a period of weeks. It's just like a fire. If you add too many logs at one time it will put the fire out. Too many people, at one time, who are **not leavened** with the heart of what you've been doing, will water it down. Let the new people who come to the meeting get in on the culture you've already established. Let them learn how to participate by catching a taste of it themselves.

This is how leavening works. It slowly takes over the lump. Pretty soon, and if you stick with it, you will begin to see some wonderful results. Eventually, whoever is willing, will be attending this *ministering to the Lord in prayer* meeting. More than likely it will not be a popular activity. The purer the activity is, the fewer people you will see attend it. The more opportunity there is for flesh, the more popular the activity will be. If it does get too big, multiply it. But you will begin to see a change in the culture of the entire group. Because you are having a focused time in the Spirit together, it will be easier for such a time to bleed over into everyday life. The entire climate of the group will begin to change. It takes months. And it takes tremendous perseverance to dig a well.

You can use well digging groups to establish a beach head in any area - prayer, worship, scripture reading, anything. But the keys are to start small, add slowly, and maintain the quality. You also have to eliminate every activity that is not the sole purpose of the group's existence. For example, if you are trying to establish a beach head of intimacy in the Spirit, don't discuss the latest football game at the well digging time. Don't hash through church problems or issues. I've been in groups where, once we've entered the room we were praying in, we had to leave every thing of earth at the door. In other words, we only allowed ourselves to speak things that were from the finished work of Christ, and from faith. This is a good discipline.

After a group has been establishing a beach head of intimacy in the Spirit, there are some practical things people can do to cooperate with intimacy and vulnerability together as a group.

1. We must learn to **see others**.

So many times we just don't notice one another. We are busy with our own stuff. Even when we encounter one another at a meeting time or a meal time, we are still consumed with ourselves. We must learn to look outside of ourselves and literally see one another. Learn to forget about yourself and your needs and completely focus on the others around you. Don't worry. God will take care of you and continually meet your needs, even when you are not watching out for yourself.

2. Learn to *value* those you see.

As you learn to look outside of yourself, seeing others is still not enough. You must also value them, treasure them, and embrace them in your heart and in deed. Everyone has tremendous value. Jesus loved the unlovable. He is kind to evil and ungrateful men. Genuinely see how important people are around you.

3. **Communicate** value to others.

Love and value has to be expressed in some way for people to get it. What speaks love to one person may not speak love to someone else. You might be trying to love others by doing and saying things that would bless you, yet no one is getting it. Find out *how to love* those around you. Ask them what speaks love to them. Universal expressions of love are always things like smiling when you see them, looking at them in their eyes, listening to them, offering to pray for them, and helping them out in practical ways.

4. **Carry** people in prayer.

When we carry one another in prayer, it knits us together in the Spirit. Carrying one another in prayer is praying for others on an ongoing basis. This is a tremendous work. It not only helps the person derive the benefit of the prayer, but it establishes them inside of you. In other words, when you carry someone in prayer, they get in you. When a group is doing this for one another, it makes for tremendous connectivity.

5. **Follow through.**

We must learn to have endurance for one another. This is accomplished by what I call ***re-engaging***. Whether we are in a time of worship, a time of prayer, or if it is in the context of a relationship, we must learn to re-engage. As distractions come (they will come) simply jump back in. It is not sin to be distracted, as long as we re-engage. As we develop this discipline in our lives, we will develop endurance and be able to run marathons in relationships and in church life.

6. **Complete the circuit.**

Open your heart wide and receive any love that comes your way. Relationships should never be a one-way street. Share your needs with others as well. Some will receive you on a deep level - most will not. That's OK. But at least be transparent with others and provide for the opportunity for the circuit to be completed.

There Is One Church In A City

In the church today we see rampant division, splits, denominations, separation, factions, schisms, and a church on every corner.

This is not the New Testament example, but we've SETTLED for it.

In fact, we expect it.

To raise a higher standard, a New Testament standard, is frowned upon. Sure, we all think unity would be **nice** to have, it's a **nice** concept – but not associated with righteousness. It is not a real standard that we uphold.

The early church did not allow for this. As you know Paul strongly rebuked the church for divisions. He said that "We should all speak the same thing…," "Be in agreement…," "Be devoted to one another…," "That there should be no divisions among you…" I Cor. 1.

Unity is not just a pie in the sky concept.

It is a command from God.

We are not allowed to remain in the fleshly condition of not being in unity. We must be diligent to preserve it. We must pursue it. And in the process, we are even more knit together.

There is only one church (everyone nod your head). The church is referred to in scripture as ONE. One entity. One thing. A unit. We would all agree with that. The problem comes in with the following question:

How do we practice unity? And better yet, how do we practice unity in this day and age?

In order to answer this, we must first see the church correctly. We must discern the Body of Christ in a correct manner.

The church is already one. There is only one Body. As Christians, there is one Spirit in all of us. We are all members of the one Body of Christ. This is true, whether we walk in it on earth or not.

As far as the practical, walking out of our unity that we already have in the Spirit...

...what are the only reasons, according to scripture, that should be allowed to separate the church?

Only 2 things:

1. Geography.

2. Not repenting of sin.

Each of these things must be looked at and understood in order to be practiced correctly.

Let's look at **geography** first.

Geography Determines What Church You Are Of

Paul wrote to the church in **each city**. He wrote to the church at Ephesus, the church at Corinth, the church at Philippi, and the church at Rome. He never refers to church**es** (plural) in a city. He only writes to the church (singular) in a city. The only time he refers to churches (plural) is in a region, such as Galatia.

It is terribly erroneous to refer to the "churches" (plural) in a city.

Let's look at a short story. I believe that if you can get the heart of this short little scenario, it will help you to see the church in a city. If you can grasp the picture, it will answer many questions.

Let's say that you went to a brand new town that has never heard of Jesus Christ and has never heard the gospel. You preach the good news in that town. People become born again. They begin meeting together in one place. They grow in the grace of God and it begins to multiply. The numbers increase. The living room is packed. It now grows to such a point that they have to meet in two homes because the one living room cannot fit everyone. Over time...three homes, then four. Occasionally, once a month or so, everyone that is meeting in different houses all get together at one time outside at a park or under a pavilion somewhere.

The fact that there are believers meeting in different locations in the city does not affect their mixing with one another during the week or separate them very much at all.

Let's look closer at what's going on...

There is tremendous overlap and an intermixing of all the families – no matter where they gather for the regular meetings.

The Smith family who attends the regular meeting at the 1201 Park Lane house often get together with the Jones family who attend the regular meeting at the 1402 Hill Rd. house. They go to different regular weekly meetings, but they still get together during the week.

Bill and Fred meet on Thursday nights at Fred's house for a "1st Corinthians 14 meeting." But Bill and Fred, along with a guy named Joe, get together for breakfast on Tuesday mornings to pray. Joe does not attend the meeting at Fred's house.

There are also several pockets of ladies from many different home meetings that get together often to visit and let the kids play together. They don't all attend the same weekly meeting either.

There is a group of guys who love to go out witnessing. They too are a combination of brothers from many different home gatherings.

The Miller family only shows up on at the I Corinthian 14 meeting on Thursday nights at the Fillmore's home, but nobody sees them otherwise. (We will be praying for them to get more involved).

<u>Everyone knows each other, fellowships with one another and is intermingled with each other on some level. Everyone is part of the same group. They just meet in different places at different times throughout the week.</u>

One Church in a City Deters Divisions

Something happens to our group in the city:

Bill and Joseph, who both meet at Fred's house on Thursday nights, have a disagreement. They try to work it out, but Bill decides that he just can't get along with Joseph and doesn't agree with him. In fact, Bill didn't really agree with how the whole thing was handled concerning the issue between him and Joseph at Fred's house.

Because of the disagreement and the way things are, Bill decides that he is going to take his family over to the Fillmore meeting on Thursdays, instead of meeting at Fred's house.

In fact, Bill is thinking of starting his own meeting. He is only inviting over to his house those who agree with him on the issue.

Uh oh. Now what?

The answer to this above scenario is <u>absolutely critical!</u> The way the church has handled this type of situation in the past is one of the reasons why we have the mess we have today. The way the church currently handles this type of situation is one reason why we keep creating more of a mess.

Division is so commonplace in the church today, that we really don't know or expect anything different.

According to Matthew 18, Bill should be pulled aside. The problem between Bill and Joseph is one thing. The fact that Bill now wants to join with another group or start his own is group is a second problem that also must be dealt with – and swiftly.

If anyone has any maturity in the Lord, they know and have tasted of God's love for the unity of the brothers. It is so dear to His heart. Jesus even goes so far to tell us in Matthew 5:23-24, *"Therefore if you are presenting your offering at the altar, and there remember that your brother has something against you, leave your offering there before the altar and go; first be*

reconciled to your brother, and then come and present your offering."

WOW!

This means that it if there is a breach between you and another, that it is more important to God that you first be reconciled and be at one with your brother or sister, than it is to come and worship the Lord! Therefore, **it is hypocrisy** to worship God and have broken relationships that you are not attempting to mend. You are living a lie. It would be like practicing murder, agreeing with it, and just allowing it be a practice in your life, while trying to have a relationship with Jesus.

If people were to practice what Jesus said in this passage, there would be no worship services held this Sunday. There would not be enough people to participate in a worship service because everyone would be too busy having important talks with people and reconciling past relationships.

Back to the story...

First Bill must be spoken to and convinced to stay and work it out with Joseph, no matter what or how long it takes. There may need to be other brothers involved to help. Both Bill and Joseph need to be willing to be wrong and have it in their heart to defer to one another.

But what if they don't work it out? What if Bill is unwilling to stay and do whatever it takes to work it out? What if he leaves, joins a new group, or starts a new one?

Because there is one church in the city, **there is no place for Bill to go**. If he goes to the Fillmore's house, Mr. Fillmore will respond with something like, "Bill, we need to deal with this thing together, you can't just join a different group."

If Bill wants to leave the church, the only way he can do it is to move to a different city. Otherwise he will be required by everyone to deal with the problem. Even if he does leave the city, we might send a letter to the church in the city where he is going.

Sin separating the Church

If Bill continues to not deal with the problem and he tries to start his own group, even after several brothers have gone to him and confronted him, the issue with Bill needs to be brought before the whole church. Eventually, if continued unrepentance is clear, he is to be officially "shunned" by the entire church in that city (for his repentance, but not to reject him). This goes for any sin in the church that will not be repented of, not just Bill's example, according to Matthew 18.

Today, the current way of the church is such that every meeting in the city is considered "it's own church." If you have a problem with one group, just join with the one next door. If you disagree with their doctrine, start your own church or attend a place with which you agree.

People are shopping church gatherings in their town like they would choose which grocery store to go to based on preferences and what it has to offer.

In I Corinthians 1:10 Paul says, *"Now I exhort you, brethren, by the name of our Lord Jesus Christ, that you all agree and that there be no divisions among you, but that you be made complete in the same mind and in the same judgment."*

Paul wrote this to the **one Church in the city of Corinth**.

I can hear it now, "Well now Terry, you're just taking this all too far…it would never work in this day and age."

If everyone would do their part, it would work in this day and age.

It is a serious thing to destroy the Body of Christ. God says "He will destroy you." To walk away from brothers and not work out a breach is damaging. The church should not allow folks to start new churches in a city. Sure, there can be more groups formed and more homes opened up because of **overflow**, but not because of disagreements. Not because you disagree with doctrine.

The Bible says that we should be in agreement. It takes time, work, talks, and prayer…and through this process the Lord knits our hearts together and makes us strong.

Remember, we must "be diligent to preserve the unity of the Spirit…". Paul tells us in 1 Cor. 1:10 that "by the name of our Lord Jesus Christ, that you all agree, and there be no divisions among you…." And he goes on to discuss the fact that the Corinthians were having quarrels and it was causing division.

There is only one church. There is only one body. I hear people all of the time saying, "our body", or "the body here", or "the body we used to belong to." This is all wrong. To say such things exposes a lack of really seeing the church. It is not just a matter of using the wrong word or phrase. People say these things because they do not accurately see what the church is or where it is. What comes out of our mouths is what is in our hearts. Let's don't change our words, but let's change our hearts.

Rom 12:4 *For just as we have many members in* **one body** *and all the members do not have the same function,*

Rom 12:5 *so we, who are many, are* **one body** *in Christ, and individually members one of another.*

1Cr 10:17 *Since there is one bread, we who are many are* **one body***; for we all partake of the one bread.*

1Cr 12:12 *For even as the* **body is one** *and yet has many members, and all the members of* **the body***, though they are many, are* **one body***, so also is Christ.*

1Cr 12:13 *For by one Spirit we were all baptized into* **one body***, whether Jews or Greeks, whether slaves or free, and we were all made to drink of one Spirit.*

1Cr 12:20 *But now there are many members, but* **one body***.*

Eph 2:16 *and might reconcile them both in* **one body** *to God through the cross, by it having put to death the enmity.*

Eph 4:4 *There is* **one body** *and one Spirit, just as also you were called in one hope of your calling;*

Col 3:15 *Let the peace of Christ rule in your hearts, to which indeed you were called in* **one body***; and be thankful.*

The church is so unified and one, that only geography should separate it. And geography only separates the church **as far as walking together**.

The saints in Turkey are still part of the saints in Korea. So, we must refer to the church in different regions as "The church **that is in** Korea". Just like Paul did.

A Name Is A Big Deal

Let's say for example, that we have a very large family. Their last name is Burney. The Burneys have a lot of children. Over the decades the Burneys have become so large that now there are hundreds of them. Many of them live in one particular town – Burney town. But some of them have moved away. Some of the Burneys now live in Illinois. Some Burneys live in Florida. Some of them live in New York. And, some of them now live in China.

How would we refer to the Burneys in China? Like this: The Burneys that are in China! How would we refer to the Burneys in Florida? Like this: The Burneys in Florida. The Burneys that live at 104 Main Street would be called the Burneys at 104 Main Street.

The church is the same as the Burneys. We are one family. Just like the Burneys, we are to refer to the Christians in Chicago as either "the Christians in Chicago, or the church in Chicago." If you live in Tampa, Florida, you are a member of the church in Tampa, Florida and nothing else. If we are referring to the believers in Ontario, Canada, we are to speak of those believers as "the church in Ontario, Canada."

What would happen if a few of the Burneys got angry and disagreed with the rest of the Burneys? These particular Burneys who got mad didn't agree with spanking their children like the rest of the Burneys believed. They decided that they wanted to change their name from Burney to the "Anti-Spanking Burneys." They now want to be referred to as only the Anti-Spanking Burneys. They are really just Burneys, but they have **separated themselves** by having a different name. Now, any Burney who doesn't spank, should participate with the Anti-Spanking Burneys.

Let's take a different situation. What if some of the Burneys suddenly began to disagree with the rest of the Burneys new ways of doing things in the family? They were opposed to all the modern ways of life. They felt strongly that all Burneys should maintain all of the old Burney family traditions. Therefore, this particular handful of Burneys decided to form their own group and change their name to the "Traditional Burneys."

What if some Burneys got together and changed their name based on what job they had or based on where they lived or based on how many kids they had? This would all seem like nonsense. In fact this whole example is nonsense. Why would any Burney want to do such a thing? To take on a different name than the family you really are would be crazy.

In this situation, we would have many Burneys going by several different last names. They are now separate from just the Burneys. They all are separate from each other, and they only associate with each other. Now, there are different Burney family reunions. There are now different Burney family picnics. They've all taken on different names based on disagreements and based on what they believe or don't believe. **These names identify them, align them with those who believe the same way, and separate them from those who do not.**

Really, the only thing that makes a Burney, "a Burney," is the fact that they have Burney DNA. It's the fact that they have Burney blood running through their veins is what makes them a Burney. If a Burney had different views from another Burney, they would really still be a Burney. If a Burney had any number of various beliefs, moved to China, or even changed their name; they would really still be a Burney. What makes them a Burney is physical in nature and **cannot be changed**. It does not matter if they distance themselves and identify with being an Anti-Spanking Burney, what makes them just a Burney is still flowing through their veins.

The same is true of a Christian. We are only to be followers of Jesus and nothing else. We are only to be Christians and nothing else. What makes a Christian a "Christian" is something that is in our spiritual DNA. It is because of something that is running through our spiritual veins. What makes us Christians is the reality of the Spirit of Jesus Christ living inside of us. We are Christians because it's **who we are**. We are Christians because of a relationship we have with Jesus. It does not matter if a Christian believes in once saved, always saved, predestination vs. free-will, pre-tribulation, post tribulation, mid-tribulation – none of these things changes **who we are.** There is only one thing that makes us Christians and that one thing is what unites us and makes us one Body. Yet, Christians align themselves and separate themselves with others who "believe like they do." Christians take on different names, separate themselves, and group themselves with others based on things that have nothing to do with what makes others a member of the Body of Christ or not.

We all have a strong need for identity. Who am I? Who are we? Groups have strong needs for identity other than the identity of the church in the city. Individuals have strong needs of identity other than just "Christian", or "follower of Christ." It's all too vague for us. To be just a part of the church in Chicago is too general for us. It requires too much faith. It's too hard to relate to. All we are able to relate to is divisiveness. It's all we understand. We are eagles who have been born and bred in captivity.

Names divide us. Or, a name can unite us. When you take on a name for the group that you are with, at the very moment you do this, you separate and distinguish yourself apart from all the other believers who are not of that same name. You also just aligned yourself with everyone else **who is** of that same name.

A name provides identity. It provides belonging.

Don't EVER give the people you are walking with a name. It is completely unbiblical. All you are is the church in …. whatever city or town or province you are in. You are a Burney! You are a Christian, and that's it.

We are not to recognize denominations. The word denomination means "to divide". In a mathematical fraction like 4/12, the bottom number is the denominator. This is the number you **divide** by.

Do you think that after the judgment, when we are in the Kingdom of God together, that God will refer to the Baptists? Will He refer to the Methodists? Of course not. So why do you do it now? **Why**

not stop doing it? Stop contributing to division and recognizing groups and names. Stop calling your group by a name. It's unbiblical. You are just the Christians in whatever city or town you are in. You may refer to yourselves as "the saints that meet at such and such place," just like Paul did. If you don't, you are dividing yourself from those who are not of your group. There is only one group in any city…you all just happen to meet at different times and at different places.

This exposes the division in our hearts. In your city, do you feel like the saints that meet at the Baptist building are a part of your group? They are. It's just a different meeting. You must change your heart on this. There is one church in the city, but different meetings. The Christians at the "Baptist meeting" may not know that you both belong to the same church. But you can know the truth. Do you feel like the Christians who meet at the Lutheran building in your city are a part of your group? They are. But they don't know it. They just refuse to meet with you because you don't share their name. As we all begin to relate to one another and see one another according to what the truth is it will change our practice, our minds, and our hearts. It will change everything.

Where to Go From Here

It's difficult to create unity out of disunity. I realize it is next to impossible to try to get a divided church in a city to come together (to truly come together). I'm not saying God can't do it or He won't, but it would take Him doing it and it would take many people doing their part. People's mentality and total way of life here in the West consists of division. It is ingrained in our society. We have hundreds of years of independence rooted in our genes. America was founded upon "The Declaration of Independence." *Unity* is a common word but the true and heart level spiritual meaning is completely foreign to us.

Doing unity-type activities, such as holding events in a city for all "churches" to attend, things that appear to be steps of unity, usually only give the appearance of unity. As long as everyone is a part of a "church," we really cannot achieve true unity. As long as people ***belong*** to a traditional organization with a name, they will be separated (at some level) from those who are not of "their church." Please understand me. There is nothing at all wrong with walking closely with a group of people. You can only walk closely with so many. God will have you with a certain number of people. You will be knit with them and committed to each other. There is nothing wrong with acknowledging that. However, belonging to an organization is not OK in the church. It's fine for a baseball team, a fraternity, or a social club. There is nothing wrong with institutions, systems, or organizations – in things of the world. But God's church is not a thing of the world. It is not to be institutionalized and changed to fit men's ideas. If to an organic and living church we dictate a series of predetermined events, it will become largely dysfunctional. This is what we see today.

When you join a club, an association, or a fraternity, you are separating yourself from those who are not of that club. And that's perfectly fine in things of the world. Those who are members of the "Lions Club" are included with those of the Lions Club. Those who are not members are not, and for a reason. But we should not take on different names within God's Church. You are separating yourself from those who are not of that same name.

The problem is most everyone that belongs to a traditional church has a "golden calf", but they don't see it as that. They would feel like they are losing something or going against God in some way to actually take down their sign and to forsake their name (the name of their organization). But it would take those type actions to get back to the scriptural example. You cannot have true unity if everyone in a city just comes together occasionally and has an ecumenical meeting. The ecumenical movement is not unity. Many times it can even be an expression of humanism.

We cannot make attempts to come together as a church in a city and then go back to our individual "churches" on Sunday. We cannot each maintain memberships in religious organizations and then try to be one church in a city. The identity we each have with "our church" is too strong.

The easiest way is to leave the traditional churches, forsake the names, and meet in simpler ways. If you stay with your religious affiliation and name, you are practicing division according to I Cor. chapter 1.

What Can You Do About It Now and Today?

First, change your heart. In your heart, you need to stop belonging to a "church." Change your belonging to the church in the city you live in. *I am not saying you should forsake the people you are with or your commitment to them*. But you need to repent of being a member of an organized, traditional, non-profit, religious institution. The scripture forbids it (I Corinthians). It fosters and promotes division in your city. No matter how involved your church may be with other groups, the name they maintain is still providing an identity that is divisive.

I know those are all strong words, and you may not fully see it yet, but at least spend some sincere time in prayer about all this.

What does the Bible say about belonging to a name that is a name separate from your other brothers and sisters?

Look again at what Paul said in I Cor. 1

"Now I exhort you, brethren, by the name of our Lord Jesus Christ, that you all agree and that there be no divisions among you, but that you be made complete in the same mind and in the same judgment. For I have been informed concerning you, my brethren, by Chloe's people, that there are quarrels among you. Now I mean this, that each one of you is saying, "I am of Paul," and "I of Apollos," and "I of Cephas," and "I of Christ." Has Christ been divided?"

How much more plain can it be?

We know the truth, but we lack the courage.

I know it is a high calling, but from the New Testament example and commands, you are required to do this or some form of this:

1. Go tell the Christians that you associate with and your "pastor," that you believe there is only one church in your city. Tell them you believe the name of the church and denomination affiliation is unbiblical and is a divisive practice. You still want to fellowship with them (at whatever level you can after repenting of all this),

but you can no longer be a member. You are a member of the church in the city and you became a member of the church when you accepted Christ. Any additional membership requirements are the inventions of men, are not Biblical, and promote division in the Body.

2. Urge the saints you are with to take down their sign on the building. If God wants to add to the number of Christians who meet with you, He will do it with out having a store front display.

3. Try to get others to meet with you someplace outside of that religious building and not on Sunday, to get all the religiousness out of your system. Quit dressing up in fancy clothes and having "services" (that's not what the Bible calls a meeting of the saints anyway, it's another tradition of men).

4. As you get free and begin to truly see the church, go and visit regularly all the different meetings in town. Remember, those are just meetings, not churches. Don't be divisive, sectarian, and just attend home meetings. You should regularly visit with the other saints in your city and go as far as they are willing to go but without going against scripture. Meet with them, invite them over for supper, and recognize them as part of the group. You are all one group in the city or town that you are in (even though that may not be in other people's hearts, you can choose to live the truth).

5. If someone asks you in your city, "What church do you go to?" Tell them you are a member of the same church they are a member of.

"The Church that is in Their House"

There are a few references in the New Testament that Paul makes saying "the church that is in their house," (Rom 16:5, 1 Cor. 16:19, Col 4:15). If you read those verses from a bias and a preconceived idea of there being many churches in a city (a bias that Paul did not have), then you might say that these verses are indeed evidence of there actually being multiple churches in a city.

Because such a thought is not consistent with the rest of Paul's language throughout the New Testament, this would not make any sense. The more accurate way to read these verses is to understand that Paul is simply referring to Christians that meet or gather in those particular homes. It does not mean they have their own identity or their own name that is separate from the rest of the church in that city. Multiple Christians in any setting can be referred to as "the church." Paul is not coming from a bias of division that we all tend to have. Therefore, he would not be stating that the Christians that meet at those particular homes are an entity in and of themselves, or who are separated from the rest of the Christians in the city and who have their own boundary. If you understand that there is only one church in any city, then there would be no problem using such language as Paul did.

If you can follow this example closely it will help. Let's say that we have a baseball team called the Tigers. On game day, some of the

Tigers are on the field warming up. Some of the Tigers are taking batting practice in the batting cages. And, some of the Tigers are in the locker room. If you wanted to refer to the Tigers that were in the locker room, you would say, "the Tigers that are the locker room." This would not make the baseball players who are in the locker room their own team. The "church that is in their house," simply means, the "Christians that are at their house."

Miraculously, I recently got many church leaders together in my town. We had a big fish fry. I spoke on everything I've been talking about here in this chapter. I showed them from the scriptures how they needed to take their signs down in front of their buildings and let go of the names that divide us. They all said "AMEN!" Yes, they really did. I was so excited! After that meeting, I pursued them and called them, but I never heard back from them.

All we can do is our part. Jesus said that He would build His church.

One last note on this subject:

Don't obtain a tax exempt 501c3 status.

You are not a business. And the group you are with is not an entity in and of yourselves. When you get a 501c3, you are saying that your group is *a thing*. It is saying you are an article, a unit, an item, in and of yourselves. This is not so. Having a name for your group does this as well. The folks you happen to meet with, walk with, share life with are just that – people in the city that you are sharing life with. The church is organic, ever growing, changing, overlapping and alive. Do not create an artificial boundary other than that of geography. Don't create an artificial boundary and identity around those you are walking with by obtaining a 501c3 or by having a name.

Remember, you all are a part of an entity that is much bigger than yourselves. You are part of a unit, a thing that does have a name. A name which is called by the church in whatever city or town you are in. To get a 501c3 is saying that the folks you are walking with have their own identity. This will tempt you in your hearts to view yourselves that way. We are trying to get back to Biblical reality. Let's don't do things that make it more difficult.

Jesus said, "Woe to you if all men speak well of you".

In other words, if you are going to live according to the New Testament and the teachings of Jesus, it will cost you. It will cost you everything.

It takes courage, but don't be afraid! Others are doing this all over the world! I hear from people every week through email, who are forsaking the divisions of traditional church and are meeting with only the identity and name of Christ as one church in a city.

Now it's your turn.

Preserving Unity and

Relating To One Another

The church of Jesus Christ is to be organic. It is not a rigid machine with an agenda, but a living breathing organism. We are the Body, building itself up in love and edifying one another.

Unity is so strong in God, but yet it is so delicate if not nurtured.

Division is rampant in the church today. Brothers are not speaking to one another. There are offenses, hurt feelings, and distrust. How can this be? More importantly, how does it start and how can we prevent it?

Division starts so very subtly among us. It starts as a minute and tiny morsel in the heart. It starts as a slight disagreement or a seemingly insignificant offense. It is then that the foundation for a judgment begins to take its shape. The subtle attitude that is the beginnings of division says, "That brother or sister is like that, or they are like this. They treat me like this or always say those kinds of things." Pretty soon, your behavior towards them is a little distant. Instead of dealing with it in your own heart and going to them, you ***talk about them*** to someone else – a poor decision, so it spreads.

Soon there is division in the body. Don't be unaware. If God has delivered you from the traditional way of meeting, Satan will surely want to bring an assault. This is our very enemy. How do we combat such a slippery and common enemy as division?

Paul encouraged us to be diligent to preserve the unity. How? Unity is preserved by each individual member (that's you) being strong in the very basics of the Christian faith - forgiveness, speaking the truth in love, bearing with one another, patience, and suffering with one another.

It is critical that we recognize the fact that our brothers and sisters around us are weak. You are weak, I am weak, we are all full of weaknesses and error. We cannot be offended by weaknesses. Perhaps the brother didn't know any better. Perhaps God hasn't revealed this or that to them yet. Maybe they had a revelation at one time in their lives of how to conduct themselves in a certain situation, but they forgot. The thing you are offended by in your brother; is something you also do - or have done at one time or another. Can't we forgive? ***Can't we always hold that brother or sister as being dear in our heart, even if they made a mistake?*** Aren't they worth going and talking to them about it? We must learn to give each other plenty of room.

The very subtle hurts we receive from one another – which happen constantly - are the very building blocks for self protection and judgments among us, all leading to division in the church. It is imperative that we are extremely diligent to deal with hurts quickly, forgive, hold that brother close, and not self-protect or distance ourselves. If we are ever offended and avoiding someone because of it, we are obligated by the Lord's command to first deal with our own heart by forgiving them, then embrace them in our hearts, and if necessary, go work things out. This should be done much more often then we might think.

If your hand got an infection, would you cut it off as quickly as you could? If your child offended you, would you disown them? We must come to a place of knowing of the treasure that is in one another. Yes, your brother is a treasure! You are to treasure him as much as you do your very hand. He is Christ's hand. He is your hand. "We are members of one another." Your brother or sister is as close to you as a child or blood family member – even closer. How is it that we tend to discount one another so quickly? We can't. We must gain and understand our true identity. We are all one thing. We are one entity, one temple, one organism. It is not optional to walk away. Unity MUST be preserved because if you reject your brother, you are doing it to yourself and to Christ.

The Lord's command in 1 Corinthians 1:10 is that we all agree and speak the same thing. This is to be pursued. However, it is also true that unity is something of the Spirit that has already been accomplished. From Ephesians 4, we see that it is something to be preserved. There are many things that are already true and that are already accomplished in the spirit, in the heavenly places, and from the *finished work* of Christ. Yet at the same time, we do not fully see these things manifest on earth in all situations.

For example, the scripture teaches that we have all of the righteousness of God in Christ, yet on earth and in these bodies we still sin. The scripture tells us that we have the mind of Christ. This is true. However, all of our thoughts are not God's thoughts. We see from scripture that we are in Christ and seated at the right hand of the Father, yet you are reading this book and your feet are still on the earth. The same is true for our unity. We can see from Ephesians 4 and all throughout the New Testament scriptures that there is one body and we are one in the Spirit. This is already done and accomplished in the heavenly places. However, we are commanded **_to preserve_** this unity. We are to all speak the same thing, we are to be in agreement, and there should be no divisions among us.

I can disagree with my brother on a doctrinal issue and still experience being one with him in the Spirit. There can be tremendous love, respect, and unity, even if we disagree. Don't get me wrong, we are never to "agree to disagree." We are commanded from scripture to talk through and work out our differences. Some conversations may last for five years! We will have on-going issues that we disagree on in which we are trying to find the truth together. However, we are never to separate because of doctrinal differences. Only sin or geography should separate the church.

We should never try to achieve unity by agreeing on doctrine alone. We should always begin with the truth that is in the heavenly places. We should begin by believing the truth that we already are one in the Spirit. If we believed this, it would take care of so many other problems. If we truly see and believe that we are one - that we are family, then arguments and disagreements could never separate us. Our family may hurt us. We may get knocked around. But we will always come back to the dinner table because we are family and we see ourselves that way.

If you have a natural family and they believe they are a family, they may have sharp disagreements, but they still are family. They will still live in the same house.

Suppose you had a very sharp disagreement with someone and you could not get along. And suppose that you were not family and that you were not one with them in any way. Then you would more than likely just go on your way and probably separate. ***It wouldn't be worth the trouble.***

This is what we see in the church today. We are not worth the trouble for one another. If we don't get along with someone or some group, we just go to the next one. This is an abomination. This promotes division in the church. We tend to only want relationships that are convenient, easy, and relationships that make us feel good about ourselves. We really don't want to do much work when it comes to relationships.

The reason why we separate so often from each other is because we have an ***identity problem***. We do not believe that we are one in the Spirit with one another. We do not believe that we are really one body. If we truly believed that we are one family with those in the church, we would never let any disagreements or hard feelings separate us. But, as hard as it may be, we would do whatever it takes to work through it.

When the Going Gets Tough, The Religious Get Going

Home church will expose you. If you stay in a house church setting for very long, you will get to see what your foundation is all about.

The churches in the New Testament were home churches. They had all sorts of problems. There was sin in the church that had to be dealt with. They also had arguments, divisions, hurt feelings, offenses, disagreements, and disputes. All of these problems are addressed in the New Testament letters.

The point is that you will probably see more problems come to the surface in house churches than in traditional church settings. Why? Because in the traditional church setting you are allowed to attend and you don't really have to get to know anyone. In traditional church settings, many problems and personal issues that people have go unexposed, unnoticed and undealt with. People can sit on a pew and listen to a message once a week and have all kind of trash going on in their lives and know one knows the difference.

When you are part of New Testament church life, it gets more personal. You will get together with people more often than just the weekly meeting. You get to know each other. You get to really enjoy the gifts and the good things that others have to offer. You also get to see each other's bad points. That's why house church settings are places for explosive growth. You get blessed and loved on quite a bit, but everyone gets exposed and confronted on their weak points. It's how true growth occurs.

Being exposed and confronted is really a wonderful thing. It is God's love for us. "He disciplines those whom He loves." To be confronted is not negative, if it's done properly. Many people's idea of being exposed, confronted, or reproved on their sin is very negative. This is often because people have confronted others sharply and with rejection in their heart. Or, confrontation has taken place when there has been no firm foundation of love and total acceptance "no matter what."

A brief aside on confronting others: We should always confront as though we were *coming along side* the other person, as opposed to *a head on collision*. Confrontation is always to be done in the heart of wanting to be a help and an aid to the person we are confronting. When you confront someone, try asking a question about their practice to give them the benefit of the doubt. Ask them, "Where were you coming from in doing that?" People must not ever feel attacked. When people feel attacked, they defend, they react and they fight back. Always reassure your love for them **many times** in the middle of a talk like this. People are extremely delicate and very skittish, even if they don't show it.

Religion has often been a place for people to hold strong opinions and then to reject others who do not hold to those same opinions. If we want to be followers of Christ and not be religious, love and truth must always go together. If we hold to the truth without love, we are fleshly and we will cause damage. If we love without holding to the truth, it is not really love at all.

As you are in a house church setting, you will get to know one another. People's junk will eventually come to the surface. When this occurs, something great will happen! Everyone will get to see how real their Christianity really is.

Will you forgive that other brother, even though they have a sin or weakness in their life? Will you speak the truth to them, or will you ignore the sin so as not to cause an offense? Will you pretend their sin or weakness is not there so you don't have to deal with it? Will you receive reproof if you are confronted concerning sin or error in your own life? Will you receive reproof if accused unjustly? Will you hold an offense? Will you come to the light? Will you blame others? **Will you do what ever it takes, no matter what, no matter how long, to work it out and to stay in the light so as to remain being one with your brother or sister?**

Traditional churches, of course, have relationship problems just like anywhere else. People get offended, then they leave, and then they "join another church." Because of the strong marketing efforts traditional churches do with signs, buildings, ads, and programs, the traditional church is able to have a steady influx of new folks all the time to keep the whole show going.

Home church is not that way. Because of the small numbers, if two or three families get offended and leave, you just took a pretty good hit.

In my experience of home church, there have been seasons when I've been with multiple families, and seasons when I've only met with a few. People come in and out for all sorts of reasons. People move away, people go back to the traditional organizations, or they leave for what is the most common reason…

…If you are being real and honest with one another, the water will sometimes get hot in home church. Those who have a solid foundation of forgiveness, perseverance, love for the truth, and fervent love and devotion to one another, are the only ones who can really make it through relationship trials.

The scripture says in Romans 12:10 to "*Be devoted to one another in brotherly love…*" **If you are not devoted to one another, you will never make it.** You will wind up back on a pew somewhere with shallow, more palatable relationships. If you want to really live a life of independence from other people, do your own thing, and just attend a meeting in a home, your motivations will ultimately be exposed in a fully functioning home church setting.

People everywhere are in different places in their faith. People will want to have church in homes and non-traditional settings for many different reasons. Some are rebels. Some only want to share their opinions and be heard. Many can not fit in or be accepted in the traditional setting so they attend a house church as an alternative. Some meet in homes because it's cozy.

The vast majority of people, whether it's home church or traditional church, are gathering together for reasons other than a love for Christ.

Many times these folks don't even see their own motivations and would confidently assert that they are coming together only out of a love for Christ. ***But time always tells us a great deal.*** When things get difficult or if there is confrontation involved, people's foundations all come to the surface. The religious, the game players, and those who don't have what it takes for body life will eventually leave.

Usually, they will slowly quit coming and you will never see them again. Or, they'll make up an excuse. They are usually not of the quality to speak to you in person concerning the truth of how they really feel. They don't have the courage or the faith to announce their departure in a proper way. Nor will they do what it takes to work it out.

It is not necessarily a bad thing that people leave.

"They went out from us, but they were not really of us; for if they had been of us, they would have remained with us; but they went out, so that it would be shown that they all are not of us." 1 John 2:19

As a group, you will see the Lord prune you back and actually "weed out" those who never had the New Testament heart and convictions for gathering in the first place. Then, as you keep your homes open, practice true hospitality and continue to gather together, more will come around as time goes on.

Quality comes out of quantity. As the numbers grow and new folks beginning meeting with you again, some of those will leave as well. Although being a part of a large fellowship of multiple families has its advantages, I am perfectly content to meet with just a few. The quality is usually there. Those few people usually are your core group who really want to be there and who really want to share life together.

Hospitality Is a Rare Find

A few people wind up visiting in the front yard of Sam's house one evening. Janis, Sam's wife, yells out to Sam from the kitchen window, "Supper is ready Sam." Sam says, "Hey guys, I've got to get inside. Supper is ready. See you all next time."

Excuse me. Umm, Sam? May I make a suggestion? Let's try that again.

Rewind.

A few people wind up visiting in the front yard of Sam's house one evening. Janis, Sam's wife, yells out to Sam from the kitchen window, "Supper is ready Sam." Sam says, "Hey guys, come on in and let's eat."

This is called *hospitality*. It is absolutely **vital,** in New Testament church life. Without hospitality, we are left in isolation from one another. Without hospitality, we are cold towards one another. Without hospitality, we largely remain separate and alone in our homes.

Hospitality is rare in the church here in the Western part of the world. The hospitality we do have is poor, shallow, and lacking. In my travels to Mexico, I've experienced far more hospitality from unbelievers, than I have from most Christians who are here in America. In fact, I believe that generally speaking, the poorer people are financially, typically the more hospitable they tend to be.

Hospitality is a foundational stone for New Testament church life. Without it, we don't have much to build with. Without hospitality, the majority of our efforts to experience body life with others will be short circuited.

What is hospitality? The New Testament scriptures use the word hospitable about six times.

"An overseer must be above reproach, the husband of one wife, temperate, prudent, respectable, hospitable, able to teach," (I Tim. 3:2, Titus 1: 8). Most of your "so called church leaders" today are not qualified to lead because they are not hospitable. Being hospitable is not just having some people over for an occasional cookies and punch, as we will see in a moment.

"Be hospitable to one another without complaint," (I Peter 4:9).

"Contributing to the needs of the saints, practicing hospitality," (Romans 12:13).

This scripture in I Tim 5:10 defines which widows are to be put on the list to receive help from the church *"...if she has been hospitable to strangers..."*

"Do not neglect to show hospitality to strangers, for by this some have entertained angels without knowing it," (Heb. 13:2).

The Greek word for hospitable in the New Testament is *philos.* Which means, "beloved, dear, or friendly"

Let's look more in depth at what is at the heart of being hospitable so we can understand how we can actually practice it.

Let's look at how Paul felt about the saints in Philippi. In Phil. 1: 8, he says, *"For God is my witness, how I long for you all with the affection of*

Christ Jesus." The Greek word for affection is splagchnon, which literally means *emotion from the inward parts.* Paul loved the Philippians. He **felt** emotion and love for them. He **longed** for them. Today, especially in the West, we have become very afraid of being in error because we don't want an unhealthy charismatic emotional experience. Therefore we have largely rejected any feelings of emotion as being Biblical.

It is important that we *long to be with* one another. It is important that *we feel* something for one another. I Thessalonians 2:8 says, "*Having thus a fond affection for you, we were well-pleased to impart to you not only the gospel of God but also our own lives, because you have become very dear to us.*"

Our love should not be cold toward one another. But if we do love one another, it should be expressed in very practical ways. When you have visitors over to your house, give them the best food you have. Learn to cater to people. Hospitality is lavishing on one another and pouring out on one another. Give unreservedly, your house, your food, and your time. If someone is over at your house visiting and it begins to get late, offer for them to spend the night. If they say "yes", insist that they take the finest bedroom in the house. Give your company the choices cut of meat at the dinner table. Keep their drink glasses full, without them asking for a refill. Fill their dinner plate with seconds and don't wait for them to ask. Give, pour, and wait on them.

Stop Being Selfish

Most people are extremely self-focused and self absorbed. The vast majority of people are usually only interested in themselves. Sad to say, this is true for a lot of Christians as well as non-Christians.

Have you ever observed people have a conversation? Almost always, no one really listens or is interested in what the other person is saying. Each person is just waiting for the other person to finish so they can get to say what it is they want to say. Everyone wants to talk about themselves. Rarely, is anyone genuinely interested in the heart and mind of the other person. And if they are, their interest and attention span is severely short. You must learn to stretch and grow in not being so selfish in conversation.

It is a learned art to love people in conversation and be able to effectively draw out their heart to love them. When you talk to people, ask them questions about them. Ask your visitors personal questions to draw out their hearts. Ask them how they are doing. Ask them about their day. Ask them about **how they are doing in their heart**. That is a very important question that you should get used to asking people very often. It is very rare for someone to ask someone else how they are really doing in their heart. Also, ask them about their spouse and children. Many of these questions will spawn three or four more questions you can then ask about them. Look the other person right in their eyes and see their heart. Be filled with love, compassion and genuine concern for them, their plight, and their life. At any one time, you should be able to spend at least 30-45 minutes talking, sharing, asking questions and being completely focused on the person in front of you. This will love others and build them up. Others need to feel known and heard. Just think if someone else loved you in this way a couple of times a week.

As you invite people into your home, give them the best meal you can afford, love on them by making their heart and life the focus of the conversation. Pray for them, and when they do leave, send them on the road with extra drinks and a snack for later. Do this and you will edify the body of Christ. Be sure to invite them over again. Have a big heart.

2 Corinthians 6:11-13 says, *"Our mouth has spoken freely to you, O Corinthians, our heart is opened wide. You are not restrained by us, but you are restrained in your own affections. Now in a like exchange – I speak as to children – open wide to us also."*

This is heart language. This is affection. Out of this longing and love for one another, comes pure hospitality.

Let me ask you, how many books do you have on your shelf? How many hours have you spent reading those books? How many hours have you spent listening to Christian tapes, teachings, and lectures? In contrast, how many hours have you spent **having people in your home**?

We seek information and knowledge more than walking out what the scripture says to do. Give people your bed, your time, and your food, instead of digesting more information and teachings. We need to live life instead of constantly dissecting *how to live life*. We'd rather study *about* the life God has given us, dissect it, and examine it, rather than live it and enjoy it. It's all disguised under the mask of gaining more truth. We are *"always learning, but never coming to the knowledge of the truth,"* (2 Tim 3:7).

We often feel like we have nothing to give. We are too tired. We are too spent. We are too broke. This is why you are tired, spent and broke. It's because we are mostly selfish. If you learn to give, you will be strengthened. God will give to you so you can give away to others. When you stop giving, you cut off the flow. Spend plenty of time in prayer with

God and learn to receive love from Him directly. As He strengthens you in the inner man, give it away to others.

"What if we don't have enough food?" Learn to stretch it or pull something else out of the pantry. Be flexible and adaptable. If you absolutely don't have the food, invite people over and have them bring their own food. No big deal. Talk to your spouse and prayerfully come to agreement on being hospitable. You will help change the culture and climate in your fellowship. When you get multiple families practicing real hospitality – congratulations! You've just entered a common experience of New Testament church life!

Larger Gatherings, Hierarchy, and the Cell Church Movement

What happens if you are suddenly packing in 40 to 50 people in a home for a meeting? It's time to consider having more than one meeting. Remember, in body life, you are getting to be with the saints and spend time with them throughout the week. If you are not meeting-focused, but relationships throughout the week are driving the church, then having different meetings at different houses throughout the week is not taking away from anything. However, if the weekly meeting is all you are doing, it will be very hard for you to want to break it up. We'll call it multiplication instead of dividing.

If the group or network of believers you are with begins to get very large, it is important that you all come together with everyone on occasion. I would suggest that once every two weeks or at least once a month you all gather together at a park, meet under a pavilion, someone's back yard, or occasionally rent out a community facility if you must.

At times like these, it's important how you physically set up the room because you are not in someone's house. You never want to go back to the pulpit / stage / pew format because you have a large group meeting. For example, instead of having the chairs in rows all facing one direction, arrange the chairs in a circle. You may have to double or triple layer the circle. You can even have a table in the center with some wine and some bread for different ones to partake of at any point during the time. Encourage people to come up and have the wine and the bread whenever they want to during the time to remember the Lord's death and resurrection. The point is that in large meetings, stay away from religious trappings and the old mentalities like having a stage up front with a worship team. This is not conducive to different ones leading out with songs and group participation. We don't want chairs facing a stage or a worship team because we are not focused on a worship team or any one person. It's the body that is edifying itself. We are focused on Christ and Christ who is in **all the people present** at the meeting. If someone has an instrument to play, let them play it while they are in their own seat. If you have several musicians, let them be behind the circle. Pass out song sheets instead of using an overhead projector.

I know this all may sound really nit-picky. But let me explain why this is important. There are so many things that we associate with "church." Some of these things are not bad **in and of themselves.** But very subtly we can revert to a way of thinking that causes us to lose the organic, the spontaneity, and the freedom that we should all have and are trying to gain.

Although the Lord will always have us with a core group that we are committed to and devoted to, as mentioned before, I do visit various traditional meetings on occasion because it's important that I meet with others in the city. We all are members of the same church, whether other people know it or not.

As I attend these traditional meetings, they are all **set up** the same way – chairs in rows facing a stage, worship team on the stage, overhead projector, and a lecture podium. What's the problem with having all these kinds of things in a large meeting?

All of these things throw the group into feeling like they are "in church." Every traditional meeting I attend feels like a church service. Because it's a church service, there are unspoken rules of what people should do in the meeting, when they should do them, and how the people are to conduct ourselves. They always have some degree of a formal feel. The Spirit of God is only allowed to flow in certain ways and in certain activities. Things are very limited. In those meetings, because we are in a church service, everyone there expects certain things to happen - and only those things happen.

The "givens" in our meetings that put us in church mode, often quench the Spirit and end up governing the time. Setting the chairs up in the typical way, passing money plates, overhead projectors, stages, worship teams, the clothes we wear, the meeting time and place, even doing the same thing every time, all contribute to this problem. Any of these things can throw us into the churchy feel. Personally, I don't ever want to meet on Sundays. In fact, the people I'm with have made it a point to not meet on Sundays at all. We don't want a churchy feel in our meetings. I don't ever want to feel like I'm going to church. We want to seek Jesus with other saints, not go to church. We've associated churchy things with Jesus Himself and He has nothing to do with any of that.

What kind of things should you do when meeting with a large group? If you are not in a "church service" many things can happen that are in the flow of the Spirit and that are spontaneous and edifying. Sometimes the benefit of meeting in non traditional ways is not so much what you do but when and how you do it. You get to do things out of conviction of heart because it's real to you in the moment, not because you did it last week.

Some examples of possible large group activities are: Worshiping the Lord, breaking up into smaller groups and praying for one another, or, someone may have a short teaching to give to the whole group. A teaching may come forth at the beginning and then you might worship with song at the end. You may not sing at all. Someone may stand up and share a testimony. It may lead to other testimonies. The whole large group may spend 30 minutes praying for only one family. A brother may gather all the men outside for a talk that is specific in charging every man to lead his household (the ladies will pray for the men while they are outside). It may be a time of healing and forgiveness where different ones approach people they need to clear things up with. As people lead out and share various things, it will inspire others to share and lead out with things. Who knows what might all happen! Let all things be done for edification.

Don't plan on having a typical music, then message following meeting. Whatever you do, avoid a canned, pre-planned church service. Stay away from the religious things that throw us into the rote, predictable, church meeting mentality. Should we pray after a message has been given? Why should you pray after the message? Is it real in your heart to do so? If it is with conviction and it is real, then pray. If not, wait on the Lord for what is real. It may take years of you having to find true conviction to get free and non-religious. Out of a reaction, **we can even become religious about trying to be non-religious.** As men of flesh, and with hundreds of years of error in our culture, it takes tremendous focus and dependency on the Holy Spirit to stay fully engaged and totally real. We have to remember that our bent will always be towards systems and methods that allow us to become passive and not active in faith on a daily basis. You may go through all sorts of gyrations and reactions to various practices. That's OK.

For example, my family and I rarely pray before our meals. Why? It doesn't seem real to me or my wife. It feels religious. But, whenever we have grocery day and my wife comes home with a van load full of groceries, we unload the van, and pile the groceries on the kitchen table. As a family, we give thanks for all the provisions. Currently, that's what is real for us. But we don't do it every time. Only when a family member has faith to pray and give thanks, do we do it. And, it may not be real and fresh forever. Being real is a wonderful way to live. The kids get to see you live out real faith in Jesus in front of them.

The Cell Church Movement

There is a definite shift in large congregations to have what are now called cell churches. For terminology sake, *cell churches* are not the same as *home churches* - although cell churches are typically in homes. Home churches are autonomous in nature. In other words, in a home church, each group is independent. Home churches are completely free to have any focus, vision, or emphasis the Lord is leading them in at any time. A cell church on the other hand, typically is an expression of a larger, traditional meeting with a definite **hierarchy** in place. The pastor provides the vision for the group and the cell group leaders carry out that vision in the cell church meetings. Cell churches can be a wonderful place of fellowship, intimacy, and connecting - and I don't speak against them in that regard. Although cell churches are the new thing, the hierarchy in the traditional church system that governs cell churches is nothing new.

Autonomy for a gathering is critical. Every home gathering is different. We all are in different places. The dynamics of those you are meeting with and are being knit with is going to change and grow all of the time. There will be different seasons with different focuses and emphasis. If the Lord wants to provide a particular focus on a particular night or accomplish certain things in the group for a season, it can easily be short circuited by the cell church agenda. Handing down the topics and subjects to be covered in the home meetings can kill the flow of life.

Of course, if those present in a particular home meeting have nothing to share and tend to not function or participate, then they would probably really enjoy a cell church and get a lot out of it. A man instituted hierarchy may seem like it provides safety, vision and promotes growth. This may be true to a certain level. But ultimately, it will stifle the church. A hierarchy is like a lid that will only allow growth and various expressions to go so far. Let me explain.

If I were part of a large group of people who all went on a trip to the planet Mars, I would definitely want a system of hierarchy in place. I've never been to Mars before. I would not know what I was doing. I would not know how to put on the space suit. I would not know what to do in the space ship, etc. I would definitely **want** a group leader to be my authority. I would need my group leader to tell me what to do and when to do it - and I would like it. I also would feel much more comfortable if my group leader was under some sort of authority as well. If I am going to a distant planet, I want my group leader to report to a project leader. And I want the project leader to be a man of great experience. If I am getting on a rocket and flying out into space, I want to know for sure that the project leader is held accountable by the science technicians and by the safety engineers. Ultimately, I need to know that someone is in charge, like a director of the space program. This man had better be a trained and licensed professional and have great experience. All of those in leadership had better be trained and licensed professionals because I certainly don't know what I'm doing in this whole situation. I would want a hierarchy to be in place, I would want to be told what to do, and exactly when to do it.

I understand that a lot of people feel this way in the church. They don't know what they are doing. The spiritual life, functioning in the church, operating in their gifts, leading their families, meeting in simple ways, and proper relating to one another **is all like a trip to Mars**. I understand that people largely want someone else to take the responsibility for them. It's just a fact of where people are at. This is largely due to the fact that we've enabled people to **stay** where they are in basic Christian skills.

The traditional church setting has largely caused the basics of the Christian faith to remain a mystery. We've not required anything of men. For hundreds of years now, the common Christian man is only required to show up to a meeting and then go home. Passivity is now engrained in our entire Christian culture. We've learned and have been trained to be dependant on an artificial and unbiblical hierarchy of man. We feel the need for this type of leadership because we've grown accustomed to others having the spiritual responsibility in the church. We all as individuals are to carry much more responsibility than we are used to having.

The hierarchy we see in the church today is not a Biblical one. Sure, in the early church there were men who led. There were people who did overseeing, but they never exercised control. Their leadership was extremely loose and hands off. The elders in a city didn't hand out a worksheet each week to all the home meetings to complete in order to make sure the past Sunday morning sermon was emphasized.

There would be no problem with a man doing the work of an apostle in a town, and a network of believers was established in that city who were sharing life together. It would be good for the man who planted the church there (the apostle) to give plenty of teaching especially in the beginning stages of the work in that city. But then he would move on to a different city as Paul did. Once the true seed of the Kingdom was planted in the city, a true apostle would not have to make sure that each house gathering was all on the same page each week. He would not have to make sure that every gathering was focusing on what he thought the weekly focus should be. The church is not to be micromanaged. The apostle Paul did however, bring correction when needed, and he provided encouraging letters of teaching that were read in all the gatherings. **He trusted the Spirit of God to grow the church.**

The gentile believers in Antioch, Syria and Cilicia were encouraged by the leading brothers in Jerusalem with this... *"For it seemed good to the Holy Spirit and to us to lay upon you no greater burden than these essentials: that you abstain from things sacrificed to idols, blood, things strangled and from fornication; if you keep yourselves free from such things, you will do well. Farewell."*(Acts 15). That's a very hands-off approach. We can trust the Lord to organically and naturally lead a gathering of saints in the way He sees fit.

Because we have created and promoted largely an entire culture of spiritually starved Christians, many believers will not feel adequate to be a part of a fully functioning Biblical home church meeting. Because true hospitality is so rare in the West, the setting of home church is difficult to maintain in our culture. If healthy, Biblical, relational church were a part of our daily climate, people would grow much faster, have confidence in functioning, and be able to fully thrive in a simple church setting without the need for an artificial hierarchy to be in place.

The cell church movement is a hybrid. It is a compromise. I think the close relationships that are developed within the cell churches are good however. But, the agenda handed down from the pastor, the hierarchy that is in place, and the name other than the one church in the city, are not good.

I've wondered however if cell churches are not the Lord's mercy in some way. Knowing how kind He is, I would not be surprised if through the cell church movement, He is shedding light and meeting us where we are as a culture. Of course, the more likely case is that the Lord is shedding light to vast numbers of people by helping them to meet in more simple, New Testament ways. And the traditional church has simply observed this and has created its own version.

I do believe that very soon (and it's already happening) as the church grows and learns how to live and function more Biblically, that we will see a mass exodus out of traditional meeting places and even the cell churches to autonomous living room gatherings throughout every city.

Why _Not_ To Meet In Homes

You should not meet in homes out of a reaction. I would say this is a huge reason, if not the biggest, for the failure of house churches.

You should never meet in homes because you are upset, hurt, mad at, or disgruntled with the people in the traditional organized church setting. But you **should** meet in homes because you want more than the traditional church system has to offer. You **should** meet in homes because you have grown in your life with God and now you are ready for true body life.

I believe that if you continue to grow, you will eventually grow out of the traditional setting. You will realize that the Lord intended more and you will want to meet in a way that is more conducive to growth and corporate body life.

As far as the Christians in the traditional church settings, they are precious and loved by God. You are to love them too. If they hurt you, you must forgive. If they burned you, you must let it go. You must be diligent to forgive, truly love from the heart, and embrace them.

You are never to have an elite attitude toward someone in a traditional meeting. Just because you may see some things they do not, does not mean that you are better than them or more spiritual. God will grant revelation and light as He sees fit. They are the servants of God.

They belong to God. He is quite able to make them stand. They are your brothers. Accept them.

As I visit traditional meetings in the town I live in, I get to know the people as best I can and invite them over. I will go with them as far and as deep as they are willing to go in the Lord with me.

I don't like the traditional meetings though. They are usually pretty bad. The meetings are usually full of error and weakness. But, so are many of the house church meetings. There are distractions, error, fleshly agendas, people quenching the Spirit (including myself) anywhere and everywhere you go. We are all incredibly weak, and God puts up with us.

We cannot choke our fellow servant who owes a little money, when we ourselves have been forgiven so much.

Does that mean that we should throw our hands up and give up? No. Does that mean that we should not attempt to walk out what God has shown us as a more Biblical way to meet and live life together? No. We must walk out what God has shown us. We must be diligent to walk in the light that we have. If we mess up along the way, we must correct it.

The people in traditional meetings are God's children (as far as we can know in any situation who really is a true child of God). We must visit with them. Those traditional meetings in your town are meetings of the church in your city in which you belong. Even though the meetings themselves are very poor, we must continue with one another as best we can.

We must forgive one another, as this is the very heart of Christianity and of the good news. *"But Jesus was saying, 'Father, forgive them;*

for they do not know what they are doing", (Luke 23:34). And in Luke 6:35, *"...for He Himself is kind to ungrateful and evil men."*

The worst thing you could possibly do is to, out of a reaction to traditional church, meet outside the traditional church exclusively and have a "better than attitude." This is horrible. If this is the case with you, please stop reading this, and repent now.

After and only after you are very clear and free from traditional church meetings, I recommend that you occasionally go to those meetings. We must always embrace our brothers and sisters who attend traditional church meetings. Don't use this as an excuse for not leaving the traditional church system in the first place because of fear of what it will cost you. You should be able to worship God with your brothers and sisters and invite them over for supper and various gatherings. Understanding that many won't come because you are not a member of their church, some will come and you can love them, and perhaps some of them will become leavened from being around you with the leaven of the Kingdom. (I understand and you should understand too, that you will need plenty of time away from the religious system to get free and to get your head and heart straight; Understand that it may take years of being away from traditional meetings to really get clear).

As you do visit the saints in the traditional setting, be sure to always maintain what you are doing with your core group of gathering together without a name, an incorporation, or a 501c3 tax exempt status. This would be you doing your part to be an expression on the earth and in your town of what God intends for His church. In the same way, you must discern the Body properly, and don't be divisive from your other brothers and sisters in your town who name the name of Jesus. You cannot separate from and not embrace people just because you disagree with their doctrine or meeting style. That would be more of the same of what the denominations and traditional church promotes.

We are not wanting to form a home church denomination, and we are definitely not wanting a group of rebels who hate traditional church people and sit around and gripe about them. Don't get me wrong, I absolutely hate the traditional church *system*. It's offensive and horribly against scripture. But I must love the people who are in the system, or else I am a hypocrite and helping no one.

I have definitely seen a lot of Christians who never really have it in their heart to meet in homes and live true body life, but they meet in homes for many different reasons. Many just get upset at organized traditional church, join with a few other upset people, and call it a home church. Really, all they've formed is an anti-traditional church. This will go nowhere. If the only bond you have with one another is a common enemy, God will not let it go very far. Usually after these types of people devour the traditional church people, they turn on each other and soon bite and devour one another.

Remember, if people ask you why you are meeting in homes, or why you left the traditional church, don't say, "Because we had a problem with a lot of things going on there." Make sure your heart is right and be able to tell people that you are meeting in homes first because it is Biblical, but also because you want more of Jesus in your life.

Drunks and Bible Teachers

New Testament body life will give you quite an education when it comes to being impressed with men, their reputations, and their ranks. Over the years, I've developed close relationships with the highly respected and the highly esteemed. Most of those are vocal people who teach. When it comes right down do it, often these men are not much different then your average drunk who is laying in a gutter.

You might take offense by such a statement. But hear me out. The drunk in the gutter lusts for another drink of wine. The respected Bible teacher can lust for position, power, respect, and control. Both are lust. The ambition of the drunk in the gutter is to get enough money to buy another bottle of booze. The ambition of the Bible teacher is often to always have an audience of people to listen to him so he can deliver his newest message. Both are ambition. The drunk in the gutter is drunk with wine and is therefore rendered useless to society. With the Bible teacher, because of his vast knowledge and understanding of the Bible, he can be filled with arrogance and pride, which renders him pretty useless as well. In fact, sometimes the drunk in the gutter is closer to the kingdom of God than the righteous man, because he knows he is a sinner.

It is not my intention to be disrespectful to people who teach. I myself teach. We need this work in the church and it is to be appreciated.

The point is that *no man* is much different from the average drunk in the gutter. I've seen that all people are pretty much the same. People just look different outwardly. Many fool themselves because they adhere to a list of Christian laws, therefore they look better than a drunk in a gutter. However, a lust is a lust, no matter what it is focused on. From within the hearts of all men proceed various forms of lusts, sins, fornications, deceit, selfish ambition, fleshly plots, unforgiveness, judgments, and lies. Some of these are polished and repackaged to look more noble and to look more Christian, which makes for the worst kind of all – religious flesh.

The Christian may have a slight advantage over the detestable sinner in that the Christian has received the grace and forgiveness of God. The Spirit of God lives in him. This gives him the opportunity to know God and commune with God. Christians have the opportunity and power to not walk in sin. But Christians don't always walk in the power they've been given. Also, all of the knowledge, Bible teaching, Biblical concepts, and information can tend to get in the way for the Christian. These things make him think that he is walking with God, when he really may be proud, hard hearted, and quenching the Spirit in his life.

Bible information and teaching can fool the Christian into not needing God. Many Christians are very religious and they don't even know it. The person who is justified and close to God is the person who screams out from the top of his lungs and from the depths of his soul and says, "OH GOD SAVE ME, I'M SINFUL AND UNCLEAN!"

The person who has all their theology straight can be in terrible danger. The person who is dependant on their beliefs instead of being dependant on Jesus is in jeopardy. The person who has memorized scripture, has extensive Bible training, has listened to years of teaching, and who has thoroughly studied the Word of God is in danger of not having a broken heart. The new believer and the sinner do not tend to have this problem. This is why so many "leave their first love" as they gain years in the Christian faith.

When the highly educated Bible people regurgitate their Biblical knowledge, people respect it. People who teach are respected. People who can talk a lot and who can explain Biblical concepts are impressive. Men who act like they know it all, tend to be believed and followed by others. We would rather eat from the tree of knowledge than from the tree of life. Knowledge, education, information and concepts are more respected and sought after than love, brokenness, hospitality, and power.

People who don't teach or say much, are usually at the bottom of man's pecking order. But those who "do", those who love, and those who serve in secret, are first in God's view. I would rather hang out with the drunk in the gutter who has a broken heart than the well esteemed Bible teacher who knows all, but practices nothing.

We must recalibrate our thinking. We must re-order our list of what is most valuable and what is least valuable. We cannot take worldly standards and make them Christian standards. The world esteems knowledge and education, but the Bible says that "knowledge makes arrogant, but love edifies." (I Cor. 8:1)

Those who teach us the Bible should be appreciated. They are not to be despised. But we need to see what's what, and in its proper perspective. Those who love us, lay down their lives for us, invite us into their homes, ask us about the condition of our hearts, are genuinely interested in us, and spend valuable time with us – **these are the ones we should gravitate toward**.

We should not be extremely impressed with those who want to do teaching among us, but don't really want to spend any time with us.

We should not be fooled into thinking that those who teach are necessarily doing some great and fabulous thing. God may use their teaching in our lives. But we must realize that many times, those who teach are not loving us or laying their lives down for us at all. Many times they are teaching us because it meets a need they have within themselves.

Many times the content and the subject matter that people teach are the things that they need most for their *own lives* – that is how they received the revelation in the first place. Often teachers and preachers hear God speak to them concerning an issue for their own life and growth, and they think they are supposed to teach it to everyone else, when really it was meant only for them. I've seen quite a consistent pattern with Bible teachers in this area. Many times their own personal internal struggles come out in their teachings over and over again, while it is all directed at their audience.

Teaching can be good. Teaching can be helpful and profitable. But we have made teaching the crown jewel of the Christian life and experience. It should not have such a place (1 Cor. 2:4). Let's don't be fooled into thinking that teaching and those who teach are something more than they are.

Love, power, kindness, and hospitality are the true commodities of the Kingdom of God. These are the commodities that grow us, heal us, and equip us. A humble person who will be a friend to you, who will sacrifice for you, who will spend time with you, give to you, speak the truth to you, pray with you, and who will receive these same things from you as well, should be worthy of much more respect and honor than the person who only wants you as an audience so they can teach in front of you.

The Epidemic Among Us

The family unit is where the strength of the church is maintained. When there are breakdowns at the family level, there is a breakdown in the church.

There is a sickness that has become so common in our families it is an accepted epidemic. It is an unseen and unnoticed plague that is destroying the very strength of the church. It is a vast and ever spreading plague in our modern society. This sickness infects the husbands, the wives, and the children. The worst part is the traditional church system offers a false remedy for this disease and allows it to go unhealed and largely unnoticed in our families. Therefore this virus continues to infect and to spread, potentially sweeping into every household in every city and every village on this planet.

What is this epidemic that has taken so many captive? What is this debilitating disease that cripples most households among us?

It is men not being men.
It is women not respecting their husbands.
It is children not respecting and trusting their fathers.
And the traditional religious system offers its counterfeit replacement.

The counterfeit intensifies the infection at the family level. The counterfeit legitimizes the disease and allows it to continue, undealt with and unhealed among us.

The apostle Paul told the Corinthians in I Cor.11 to follow in his example as he followed Christ. Immediately after he spoke this however, he said

"But I want you to understand that Christ is the head of every man, and the man is the head of a woman, and God is the head of Christ," (I Cor.11:3)

In other words, even though Paul was encouraging people to follow his example, every man is accountable to and ultimately must follow Christ and only Christ.

This scripture in I Cor.11 shows us the proper order of things. Paul was not any man's head. Paul was not any woman's head, (Eph 5:33, I Tim. 3:4-5 1 Cor.16:13, Eph 5:22,23).

Every man is to provide leadership and shepherding for his own household. Every man is to teach his family the Bible, pull them together for prayer, and actively speak into the lives of his wife and children. Every man is to provide shepherding and leadership in every way to his family, both physically and spiritually. Every man in the church is to be living an honorable and respectable life. If not, he should be held accountable by the brothers. Men are commanded to love their wives as Christ loved the church and the women are commanded to respect their husbands.

When you live with someone, you get to know them. You get to see all of their weaknesses. Women in the church don't live with the pastor and don't tend to see his weaknesses like they do their own husbands. When a wife sees her husband's weaknesses, she is tempted to not respect him. Not so with the pastor. He speaks into the lives of families without confessing his sin to them on a regular basis. He doesn't get irritated at the family, throw a temper tantrum, and then get to humble himself and apologize. The distance he has, allows him to better uphold his image of holiness. He is thought of as an extra-righteous man and he is respected as so. Why are families on their best behavior when the pastor comes over to their house? Because people believe he is in a different class than everyone else, and sometimes these men enjoy playing the part.

Many times women respect the pastor more than they do their own husbands. This is not healthy. Many times, subtly and sometimes even overtly, the woman leads the household. She also can lead the husband and the children into being enamored by the pastor. The pastor begins to have a place in the household that **only the father** should have. This is a subtle thing in the hearts of the women, in the hearts of the men and in the hearts of the children.

Often the men lack confidence, are too passive to lead, and would much rather have another man do it for them. They are quite content to let another man stand up before their wives week after week and provide the ladies with instruction and answers for their lives. The pastor is speaking more into the lives and hearts of the women than their husbands are. The women take it right in. Men can be so docile and so passive that they follow another man and allow him to lead their wives.

We've exchanged the authority structure found in the scripture of:

Christ

Husbands

Wives

For the more common authority structure of:

Christ

Pastors

Wives

Husbands

Or even the erroneous:

Christ

Pastors / Husbands

Wives

The father of a household is not to share his authority with another man.

Understood, people are crying out and begging for leadership.

But it is the man of every household who is to provide this leadership.

When one man stands before you, week after week, and speaks with authority into your life, it does something inside you. It affects your heart. Our hearts were made to follow. Our hearts were created to trust. When you spend time listening to **one man** speak, teach, and instruct, over and over again, he gets in you. You begin to trust him a little, and then a little more. This is another reason why many brothers should be speaking and teaching when we gather together.

I am well aware that many of you have your concepts all straight. "I don't worship my pastor." Or, "I would never follow a man." But I am telling you that the pastors have an unhealthy power over many, many lives.

There is a place we can give others in our hearts that has authority in us and over us. When we give this authority to people, we really listen to what they have to say. This is not ordinary listening. But listening that allows what they say to go deep into our hearts. When we give this place of authority over to people, we listen to them without their words running past our healthy filter of weighing it out to see if it's truth or not. We must remember that all men are very fallible and weak. Sometimes even quality, faithful, good men are deceitful, manipulative and selfish without them even knowing they are doing so. *"The heart is more deceitful than all else and is desperately sick; Who can understand it?* (Jer 17:9) We should never give men this place of authority in our hearts.

Only Jesus should have this place in us! Only scripture should have this place in us!

When a man speaks to us, ANY MAN, we must have the attitude of "maybe so." It must be weighed out with scripture.

If the Lord is using someone to do some shepherding in your life, you should acknowledge the Lord in this and be an imitator of their faith as Paul directed in I Cor. 11, but remember, "The head of every man is Christ." (This passage is not to be used for a fleshly *independence* among men in the church; Brothers are not to have it as their practice of just doing their own thing without an attempt to be of one mind and without an attempt to move together in unity, I Cor.1:10).

Again, there is a proper function of someone doing the work of a "pastor," which the word really means "shepherd." But if someone is doing this work and speaking into the life of a member of a family, it should be weighed out by the father of that household. The father of the household is always the gatekeeper and shepherd of the family.

Women without Husbands

What if a woman does not have a husband? What if there is someone who is not her husband, who is doing some true shepherding in her life? This is good and beneficial, as long as:

1. It takes place where there is a healthy expression of the church where many are active and functioning.
2. All things spoken are in the light with others.
3. Those who are operating in their shepherding gifts are accountable and on a totally equal playing field as everyone else (as with any gifting).

If all of the above were true, there would be a healthy atmosphere for what is spoken and shared with the singles, widows, and those without a husband or a father to be received. I've seen very healthy situations in which there was a widow or a single for whom many brothers and families provided covering and shepherding as well.

But more commonly, we have very subtly, at a heart level, substituted the place that only King Jesus should have and given that place to the traditional pastors. Because we'd rather have a man who we can see with our eyes lead us, rather than be of faith and trust in God, whom we can't see. We'd rather have someone just tell us what is and what to do, rather than seek, rather than wait on the Spirit of God. We would rather give our respect to a man who week after week proclaims God's truth to our lives from a pulpit, while we are unaware of what he does, says, and thinks during the trials of everyday life.

We want men to remain as icons in our minds, so they can remain qualified for us to follow and to trust them to provide leadership for our lives and families. If we knew all about men's real dirt, which is common to all, we might not be so impressed with what the pastors have to say. Again, if it is scripture, then be impressed. Those who lead should lead us to scripture and to Christ, not to themselves.

All men of rank should be viewed as being at the bottom with the rest of us. Those who are lowly and are of no account should be raised up. There is equality at the foot of the cross.

Romans 3:4 *"…Rather, let God be found true, though every man be found a liar,.."*

Psalms 62:9 *"…men of rank are a lie"*.

This epidemic is so pervasive and so ingrained in our culture that most will not come out of this pattern by just hearing about it or studying it. Just hearing about it and studying it will only produce limited results. As with most things, it takes living it out and learning in the reality of everyday life to really have it. It must be learned and lived with those who are already living it. Church life quickly grows the disciple. Books and articles give us concepts only. We are a concept society in a concept church. Books, articles, and newsletters flood our homes. But the reality of living the experience of church life together is rare and only for those who are sick and tired and are ready to choose more of Christ.

Tithing

The modern day organized church is kept in motion and built largely by money. Today in the church we have impressive buildings, big fancy signs, strategic locations, television ads, yellow page ads, radio spots, programs for every possible need, nurseries, salaried professionals, date night, pizza parties, youth group activities, ski trips to keep the kids happy, fancy suits, expensive audio systems, automatic retractable video screens, and million dollar family recreation centers. All of this takes massive amounts of cash. Yet without these things, the church membership would be drastically cut.

The tithe is an Old Testament requirement. But modern church teaching has twisted the scriptures and kept the tithe requirement alive in order to fund itself. *The New Testament church did not need money.* It ran on power. It ran on passion. It was kept alive and it continued to grow because of the life that it had. The modern day traditional church is mostly void of life, therefore, it has to prop itself up with hype and show in order to replace the life, in order to attract members, in order to exist. Under the New Covenant that we are in, Jesus does not require a tenth of our incomes, He requires ALL of it.

Let me explain. The large impressive buildings attract people. The buildings give the illusion and promise that there is something there, that there is something established. Think of a bank building for example.

They are fancy on purpose. They have polished granite countertops, expensive lobbies, and marble floors. Why? They do this to provide the atmosphere of wealth so that there is the "feeling" of security. You wouldn't want to put your money in a place that was built like a shack would you?

In your average traditional church today, how many people would still come if you threw away all of the extras and began meeting in a shack with a dirt floor? Or, what if we met in a park under a pavilion? No nursery or children's church. Fathers would be responsible for teaching their kids the Bible at home. Fathers would require children to sit still during a church meeting. No paid professional to bring the music, but each member would come with their hearts filled and with songs to bring. ***Who would still come if all the church had was what the New Testament Christians had?*** Without all the trappings, without the pomp and show - who would have ever attended a traditional meeting in the first place?

Shouldn't this bother us? What if a large portion of the people were only coming for all the extras? What if they were only coming for the programs? Would we really still want them to come if they weren't coming for the right reasons? Jesus knew that the majority people followed Him for the food and miracles. He turned to them and said, "Unless you eat my flesh and drink my blood, you have no part with me." Then they left. He knew they would leave. Would we ever say something that we knew would make people leave? Quite the opposite.

What should we do?

We all know about the tithe. The tithe was a tenth portion given by Israel to the Levitical priests. What about tithing in the New Testament?

There is not a direct commandment in the New Testament to pay tithes. But we do have some examples of how to relate to money and giving. Jesus said that unless you give up all your possessions you cannot be my disciple. In Luke 18:12 Jesus tells us of the man who fasted twice a week and paid tithes of all he had, but the tax gatherer who said, "I'm a sinner," was justified instead. Then there is the widow who gave very little compared to the Pharisees, but she gave all that she had. Jesus said that because she gave all that she had, she had given more than anyone else. The New Testament economy is the economy of the Kingdom of God. It's the opposite of the kingdom of man. The more you give away, the richer you are in the Kingdom. The first is last, the last first. The humble brother of low circumstances ought to glory in his high position. We don't get it though. We think that if we pay our 10% that we've covered the base and did what God expects. We are completely missing the point.

It should also be noted that a big reason for paying tithes these days is in order to fund the salaries of the leadership. If we come to a Biblical understanding of offices and gifts, we will see that this practice doesn't really make any sense. Someone who has a gift of shepherding (a pastor) is no different than someone who has a gift of prophecy, teaching, or evangelism.

Let's take a situation where we have a local brother who lives among us and shares life with us. This local brother happens to function in the gift of prophecy. Because he functions as a prophet, would we ever pool our money together and pay him a salary? What about a brother who teaches among us? Should we pay his living for him while he lives locally among us and shares life among us, just because he teaches?

Let's look at a totally different situation. If there were a brother or family among us who was **going out and traveling** to different cities to preach the gospel or function in their gifts – they are going to need money for traveling expenses. They are going to need support to cover their financial base while they are gone. These situations ought to be supported financially by the local church. I will be first in line to help support the traveling brothers.

Just like the apostle Paul (apostle means "one who is sent out") who traveled from region to region and city to city – one who is sent out, someone who is traveling, someone who is on a journey in which the sole purpose of the journey is to do the work of the Lord, these people ought to be supported in their journey by the local assembly who is sending them. But to pay for the livelihood of a brother who lives among us, just because he has a particular gift or because he teaches a lot is simply the results of a confused and contrived tradition of men.

I always like to read the epistles because in them, you can see very practical examples of how the early church lived. Paul writes at the end of Philippians that they gave him a gift to meet his needs. It seems clear that it is a financial gift. Paul also tells the Corinthians in I Cor.16 to set aside money at the first of the week so that no collections are to be made when he comes. But he goes on to explain that this money is to be sent on to Jerusalem with someone other than himself.

Paul says that those who preach the gospel have the right to get their living from the gospel…but everyone always leaves out the second part. He did not take advantage of this but chose to "work day and night" so as to not be a burden to any. This is a good heart.

In looking closer at Paul's quote of "those who preach the gospel ought to get their living from the gospel," I think that there is strong evidence that supports the fact that Paul was speaking of people like himself who are extra-local and who are actually traveling and preaching the good news. Local leaders and pastors are not usually "preaching the gospel." They are typically doing a lot of teaching, which is good and necessary, but the gospel is a very specific thing. After someone or some city has heard the gospel, they've heard it. It's time to go on to the next town or region - which is why those who solely "preach the gospel" should be offered financial support. To preach the gospel, as Paul was speaking of, has in it's meaning the traveling "bringer of good news", who would be hindered if he were to have to deal with paying for his own expenses while doing such a work.

Local brothers on the other hand, may easily operate in their gifts while working a job as well. Some may think that it would be impossible for their local pastor or leader to work a regular job while performing his duties. That's because most of the duties a pastor does are the duties of a typical business executive – which is what we've made the church to be. Marketing campaigns, committees, budget analysis, secretaries, buildings, administrative duties, etc., all are the results of us modernizing, westernizing, and adding to the church things which do not need to be.

Since we've done all of this with the church, we now have to pay someone to **oversee** all of this, which has little or nothing to do with **overseeing the lives** of the people.

The Old Testament tithe was for the priest and for the temple. Now, under the New Covenant that we are in, we are all priests. Secondly, the church has now become the temple. He inhabits **us**, not a building or a tabernacle. The Old Testament was a picture of the real thing that now is and is still to come. We don't need to pay any Levites. There are no more priests to hear God for us. We can all go to God directly. The modern day separation of clergy and laymen is a tradition of men based on the Old Testament Levitical priesthood. We are all to be just brothers with no separation of clergy. We are all clergy now. Or, you could say we are all laymen now. In fact, based on the example of the apostle Paul, the so called "ministers" we know, ought to go get themselves a job.

"What am I supposed to do with my tithe then?" people ask me. First of all you need to remove the word from your vocabulary. It is not New Testament. That's like asking, "Where are we going to sacrifice the animals now?" You are now free. Use your money to serve the Lord with however He leads you, with as much or little as you want. Give money to people who need it. Buy some tracks and hand them out on the street corner. Have a big BBQ for the neighborhood. Use it for evangelism and for giving to the needs of the saints. It all belongs to the Lord now. He gave it all to you anyway. Do with the money in your charge as the Lord puts in on your heart.

Our tendency is to assume that the principles and methods that are true in the earthly and natural economy are also true in the heavenly economy as well. However, the economy of the Kingdom of God is usually opposite that of man's economy. "The things that are highly esteemed by men are detestable in the eyes of God" (Luke 16:15). We think that because it's wise to save and stockpile money in the earthly economy that those same principles should transfer into God's kingdom as well. Jesus gave us a different example. Good stewardship in the economy of God's kingdom is to actually give your money away. Jesus did a lot of things in relation to money that speaks against the common teachings that exist today in the church. Jesus actually put a thief in charge of the money box, which would totally go against man's conventional wisdom (John 13:29). If a money plate is passed in a Christian meeting, we ought to encourage those who have need to **take money out** of the plate.

Personally, there have been times when my wife and I have given large sums of money to people. There have been times when we have given nothing away at all. The covenant that we are in only has one rule. It's the rule of love. There is only one law now in the New Covenant. It's the law of the Spirit. There is no list of rules that you have to go by anymore. God has set us free in order to serve Him in a living way.

Evangelism and Outreach

As you are being built up in your faith, it will have expression (if it's true faith). Evangelism and outreach can look very different through different people. We should never try to make others look like ourselves. There are many gifts and a variety of ways the Lord shows up in all of us. There are also different seasons with different emphasis.

The main point in this brief chapter is to tell you that having an outward focus is critically important. I believe in a healthy group, there should be an attitude and culture of working together. One of our primary purposes of being a group is in fact the work the Lord is giving us to do. There is plenty to be done. The vision of work should be part of a group's identity and their purpose for existing. Remember that the work you do in the Lord is always unto Him. Sometimes you will see no visible fruit from your labors. But on the great day of judgment, hopefully Jesus will tell you that you did it unto Him (Matthew 25:43).

The Lord will lead you into a variety of ways to be outward focused. Here are some possibilities using some of the things we've done with the folks I've walked with:

- Prison ministry: Visit the local prisons to share the gospel. You can also usually do this by getting clearance from the chaplain.

- Free Food Handout: M.R.E's (meals ready to eat) passed out on the streets, the gospel shared, and people prayed for.

- "Widows help: If you are a Christian widow or know of one who needs help, let us know. We love to do things around the house, paint, or repair things." We make a flyer with these words on it and pass it out door to door in a neighborhood.

- Home repair evangelism: Offer free services to folks for minor home repair, yard work, and painting. A great opportunity to explain the gospel. All donations rejected.

- Share the gospel doing street evangelism by passing out tracks and praying with folks for various needs they may have.

- Neighborhood cookout: Go door to door and share the good news of Jesus. Invite people to a neighborhood cookout planned just a couple of hours later within walking distance at a local park.

- Ship Bibles and materials to villages in other countries. If you don't know of any, I can put you in touch with many in need.

None of these things listed account for all the things people can do all of the time that goes unnoticed, like having people over for supper or driving across town to eat lunch with a needy soul. What about smiling and genuinely caring for the person who checks out your groceries at the grocery store?

People are lonely. Very few people are genuinely kind from the heart. A kind word, a loving smile, and genuine interest all go a long way with people. My wife has a great gift for doing this. She is a witness for Christ all of the time. Many of the people we've known or have walked with in the church have come from her just being kind to people and loving people as she goes through her day. Anytime we deliver Jesus to someone and love them from the heart, we are a witness for Christ.

A Normal Church

There is a story about a city. There is only one church in this city. In this particular town, there are anywhere from 2,000 to 3,000 people who are all part of the same church. This is an entire **network** of Christian people.

The fellowship they have with one another is completely overlapping. Every person does not know or fellowship with every other person, there are too many people for that to happen. But everyone knows and fellowships with someone, who knows and fellowships with someone else. The entire church meets and gathers in homes, in parks, in various restaurants for lunches and coffee, and often you can find them at the nearby lake for weekend camping. This vast network of people are gathering together and sharing life together in many different ways.

Seven days a week, during any evening, you can visit a number of homes in this town and find Christians gathered together. There are meetings and gatherings every single night, and you are welcomed to go to any one of them, at any time you want. They are worshipping Jesus in these meetings. They are sharing, praying, teaching, operating in their gifts, and intensely supporting one another's personal lives.

Besides the daily gatherings, about once a month, the entire church gathers together outside at the city park for a giant picnic. Everyone brings their own food. This scene is incredible. There are people scattered everywhere throughout the city park. The park is completely full of people. There are, what looks to be, about 2 acres of table cloths and blankets spread all over the ground. After a while, everyone begins to move into groups of 10 to 20 people to pray for one another. This all day meeting in the city park starts around 9:30 a.m. on Saturday morning. By 6 p.m. that evening, it is still going strong.

Around dusk at the park, there are 10 or 12 Christians still gathered around and talking on the tail gate of a pick up truck. There are 8 or 9 ladies sitting in lawn chairs together. There are still children running and playing. For the last couple of hours, there has been a children's game of kickball over at one end of the park with about 15 adults standing around visiting.

When this monthly, city wide church meeting in the park is over, everyone goes back to their homes to resume their weekly activities of work, family time, and church life all during the week.

There is nothing to identify this vast network of Christians, other than the relationships they have. There is no name of this massive group. There is no sign posted anywhere. There is no building. There is no leader. ***But many lead.***

Most of the people who want to travel to this city to visit and participate in the church activities, usually know at least one of the Christian families who live there. But even if you didn't know any of them, it is pretty easy to find them all.

You decide to take a road trip just to see what it's all about. As you drive into town, you realize you don't know where to go in order to find these Christians. Where do they meet? What time do they meet? They don't have a yellow page ad. What will you do?

It's Friday evening when you drive into town.

You stop at a local gas station and ask the clerk, "Excuse me, do you know where I would find the Christians in this town?" The lady behind the cash register replies, "Oh yea, I think a lot of them have been getting together down at the lake on Friday evenings. You could probably find them there."

You drive out to the lake. You get out of your car and discover about 20 people singing to the Lord under the stars. You join in. A brother stands up by the fire and shares a brief testimony with the group. A sister shares a prophecy. Others chime in and share brief encouragements and teachings. They begin to pray for one another. It is a glorious occasion. You've never seen anything like it. They are so free, so real, so spontaneous, and so encouraging.

When the meeting is over, several of them introduce themselves to you. They find out that you are new to the town and that you want to plug in and meet the other people in the church. They make you aware of several other gatherings that are going on the next day. Some of them ask you to join them for an unplanned, late night supper in one of their homes. You spend the late evening sharing and talking with your new friends.

The next morning is Saturday morning. You've been made aware of a variety of get-togethers you can choose to attend. There are about six people going to play a round of golf. There are a few gathering for breakfast at a local restaurant. There is a prayer meeting available in someone's home. Some of the families are going back to the lake to hang out and do some boat riding and water skiing. You don't really want to miss anything, but you have to choose. "Ok, I'll go to the breakfast. Then, I'll catch the last part of the prayer meeting."

After the prayer meeting that morning, you grab some lunch with a couple of brothers and then take a nap. You are made aware of a small gathering of Christians who are planning to meet in a home later that night to worship the Lord. You attend the worship time. Afterwards, you catch up with a group who decide to do some late night street witnessing.

Just about everyone you meet invites you into their home to stay for as long as you want. They feed you. They pray for you. They are sincerely interested in you, interested in your family, and interested in your life with Jesus.

You realize this all could go on for days. You are well aware that if you were to live in this town, there would be no way anyone could attend every gathering.

In the last couple of days, you've gotten to know a couple of the other Christians pretty well. You ask them a question saying, "What are your backgrounds?" You communicate to them how you are aware that this entire city has joined together as one church, but you would really like to know what denomination they all come from. They reply, "Brother, in our attempt to take the New Testament seriously, we've purposed in our hearts to repent from divisions and denominations. There is only one church in this city. We don't fellowship just with those who believe exactly like we do on every issue. Many of us have different convictions and beliefs on many things found in scripture, but our personal doctrines are always **open-ended** and kept open for discussion. We are devoted to one another. We are devoted to Christ.

However, we are not devoted to our own personal beliefs that are not central to faith in Christ."

"But who is **really** in charge of this whole thing?" you ask. They reply, "Jesus is in charge. You would be amazed at how well He runs the church, if people will just let Him. The church belongs to Him. He designed it, He grows it, and He keeps it - if we do it the way He laid out for us in the New Testament. Here in this city, when men started taking their hands off the church, all the gifts began coming forth. People who would never open their homes before, started opening their homes! People who would never speak before, started speaking! People's walls started coming down. People started to get honest with one another. People started functioning! It's amazing how it all came together. I have to warn you though, you can't be afraid. You have to learn to trust the Lord. If you get afraid and say that "it won't work", or from fear you revert to the old traditions of men to organize it, it will kill what the Lord wants to do. You have to let go of your personal feelings of needing to "know for sure" that you'll have leadership in place. You have to let go of "knowing for sure" things like *who you all are* as a group or where you are going to tithe to. Trust the Lord my friend, and trust the New Testament example. God gave it to us for a reason."

You realize that the example of the church in this particular city should be true for every city in the world. No walls, no one aligning themselves with a certain affiliation, but everyone belonging to the same group. And although the Lord leads each individual to be closely knit with just a few, everyone feels they are a part of one large family in this town, and they practice it.

But how did they get to this place? How did it happen?

How did they ever accomplish such an amazing feat?

It started with a few brave souls. Those who were on staff at one particular fellowship contacted the other pastors and leaders in the town. The leadership from every denomination had a meeting in that town. The pastor from that fellowship stood up and said,

"Gentlemen, we at First Methodist have called this meeting in order to share a revelation we have had. From our honest assessment of the New Testament, we find no scriptural basis to support our role of leadership at First Methodist. As men in charge of the flock, we do not deny that we do have gifts. Namely, we have gifts of leadership, teaching and shepherding. But these gifts are to be employed as any other member of the congregation should employ their gifts. We should not recognize a separation of clergy and laity or staff and non-staff.

Elders in the New Testament were given to a city, not a group within the city. Those who were appointed as elders in the early church were already elders according to the lives they lived, the spiritual qualities they possessed as men, and the spiritual authority they had that comes from God. Not because of any formal training or institutional authority. Just because a leader or pastor has a personal identity as such, does not make it so. Just because a man believes himself to be a leader, does not make him a leader. These gifts are spiritual and are from God alone. Those of us who do have gifts of leadership, gifts of teaching, prophecy, evangelism, shepherding, or apostolic functions, should use those gifts as though we were just one of the flock and in the context of just being a regular brother.

Furthermore, it has been revealed to us through the scriptures and the Holy Spirit that the management functions and administration of the church at First Methodist concerning things such as budgeting issues, buildings, the programs, marketing, and the business office functions are all in place and are a result of the traditions of men and of our Western culture. We've discovered that these things actually hinder and stifle the natural and organic functions of the people. Because we have assumed so many roles as staff members, the congregation depends on us in ways they should not. Not only has this hindered them from fully expressing themselves in their gifts and functions, but it has hindered the general edification of the church. Therefore since the church is to in essence, *run itself,* there is no need for our staff positions. We are taking our hands off the church in order to let it grow. Up to this point, we've never trusted the Lord *in the church* to grow the church. We've perceived the members as incapable, not trained, and not possessing enough spiritual maturity to adequately be a functioning church. In some ways, this may be true up front. But we firmly believe that people are to learn and grow by doing, just as we have, and that God's design and intention is for every member to have a platform and an environment to express their gifts, no matter what they may be. We have repented of our arrogance and our control, even if we had good intentions in doing so.

As of today, we are resigning. We will no longer accept a salary, but we have instead decided to get regular jobs, while continuing to function in our various gifts. Our meeting formats will also change at First Methodist in order to encourage every member to participate and bring what they have spiritually to every meeting of the church. This is consistent with 1 Corinthians 14. We still may stand up and teach on occasion, but we will encourage the others to teach as well.

Also, from the example in the scriptures, we are taking our sign down in front of the building. We will no longer refer to ourselves as First Methodist, but we will be "the Church in Bryan, Texas," of which we all are part of the same group. In fact, we're selling the building we've met in because we have no need of it. The building has been an icon and representation in our hearts of establishment, stability and growth. It has also been a perverted method of attracting members. We will be meeting in more natural everyday life settings and in our living rooms.

We realize that for you to follow us in the New Testament example in these things, that many of you will have serious concerns as church leaders. You will have concerns not only for your jobs, but also with the whole idea of how we are to meet the needs of our current modern culture. How will people in our society be able to relate to such a church? How will new people be able to come and participate? Do we not have to have the traditions we have in place in order to meet the needs of our modern society?" My answer to you men is this. Why would God establish his plain example in the scriptures of the church and how it should function, only to change it for every culture? Why would he lay out the structure of the church, which is built on the foundation of the apostles, only for every culture in time to shape it and reform it? Because of this type of thinking, we now see things like homosexuals in leadership because it is an accepted practice in our modern culture. Men, please, I appeal to you in this: *the Church should be affecting our culture, not our culture affecting the Church.*

The pattern in the New Testament is God's design. It's what works for the church. It is timeless. If we change it or alter it, we pervert it. If we pervert it to better fit our culture or lifestyles, we diminish its power and effectiveness. What God laid out for us in the New Testament is perfect. We cannot have such arrogance to say the Biblical example is no longer relevant or that it should be compromised in some way.

Men, we wonder why the experience of the early Christians is so different from ours. We wonder why when we read our Bibles it seems so different than what our real practice is, yet we have chosen to meet, to function, and to gather in ways that are so different from the blueprint the New Testament provides. These things ought not to be such great mysteries to us.

Over time, and through much talking and prayer, others in church leadership in that city listened to the brothers at the Methodist fellowship. A trend was set in the town. *By example*, the shepherds led the flock. Truly, a revolution took place in that city. All over town people began to talk about the new freedom they were gaining in Christ, and the whole thing had a snow ball effect. As people started forsaking the dead traditions of men, more people followed suit as well.

Of course, not every church leader or fellowship agreed. But over time, the majority did. Those who practiced denominationalism and division soon became the minority in the city.

Where to Start

If you are already with others, then begin with establishing some beach heads in various areas to gain ground in the Spirit. You can establish beach heads in prayer, scripture reading, worship, etc. However, you may be completely alone. Many times, people have the desire to meet in a simpler way but they aren't sure where to start.

The best place to start is with hospitality. Simply invite a family or two over to your house. It doesn't have to be a big production. It doesn't need some sort of higher approval, nor does it need to be official. You don't need to establish by-laws. You don't need to have a set agenda or a schedule. You don't even need a plan. You can even start by inviting a brother or sister over for a coffee or organize a camping trip. Build relationships that are focused on God.

The point is not how to get together with people, that's common sense. It's what to do when you are with people. Having an outgoing attitude and being somewhat hospitable will allow you to be around plenty of people. As you are hanging out with others, you have to learn how to touch the Lord together. Depending on where the other people are at in their heart and relationship with God, will depend on how far they will go with you and how long it will take. Building relationships takes time. But eventually, and if they are willing, you all can open the Bible, pray together, worship, and share hearts.

Begin by just eating supper together. Talk, visit, and share what the Lord has been doing and showing each of you in your lives. Take turns reading a few verses in a particular passage. Talk about those passages, pray together and worship with songs. After a couple of meals together, use a few of the questions in the following chapter to turn the focus to deeper things.

As you meet non-Christians in everyday life, invite them over for a monthly discussion in your home that deals with controversial issues. Questions like, "Why does God let children in poor countries starve and die? How could a loving God send people to Hell? Do you really have to go to church to go to Heaven?" Unsaved people love this kind of stuff. Over time you can build relationships. Some of them will be born again and be a part of the church in your house. You can even encourage others to open their homes so you can move around where you meet.

As you continue to open your home and others join you, over time things will change. Organically (naturally), things will evolve and change as the Lord leads. Be flexible, don't force anything, focus on Jesus, and enjoy New Testament body life!

Questions For

Group Conversations

We have used these questions to stimulate group conversation and sharing. You can use them to get to know people better and to encourage others to share on a heart level. Sometimes we will make a game out of it. You can type the questions out on a piece of paper, then cut the questions out into strips. Fold the questions and mix them up into a jar. Hand the jar to the first person in the circle and have them take out a question. After they answer their question, they have the option of passing the jar to the next person or require someone else in the group to answer the question they just answered.

Here are the questions:

What is something you would like everyone to know about you that no one probably knows?

What is the main thing the Lord has been doing in you?

What is your hope for the future in your life with God?

Name something you know without a doubt that you've experienced that was absolutely real, but that you or no one else could actually see with physical eyes.

What advise would you give to a new and eager Christian?

What is it that keeps you going everyday in the Lord?

How has your view of the church changed over the years? Your view of scripture? Your view of prayer?

You are on your death bed about to take your last breath. All of us are standing around you. What will you say to us?

What's your favorite book/letter in the bible? Why? How has it helped you?

What is your greatest on-going need you would like to share with the rest of us?

In what area do you need the rest of us to "watch your back" in?

What can you share with the rest of us in the area of dealing with fear?

Teach the rest of us what you've learned about perseverance?

Teach the rest of us what you've learned about resting in the Lord?

How has your idea of God's character changed over the years?

Tell the rest of the group what speaks love to you. How can we love you more and better?

The Most Important Thing

The point is Jesus. The point is not home church. The point is not how everything or everyone else is wrong. The purpose of this book is to shed light on some things that have been lost in the church that are hindering us. Use them and make corrections. But don't let it become your primary focus. If your focus becomes what is wrong with the church, you will ultimately wind up a dry and miserable soul.

Body life is only as good as your individual life with Christ. **Don't make the mistake of substituting relationships with people for a relationship with Christ.**

The folks who are really good at the basics of Christianity are those who live filled with the Spirit, who live full of faith, and who run their race well. Jesus is our life. Jesus is our focus. The person of Jesus is our joy and our strength. There is only hope in Jesus Christ. He has life within himself. We do not. He is not a concept or a methodology. A focus on methods and systems brings death. Concepts alone are empty and lifeless.

True growth in God comes through suffering, through pain, and by staying broken at the feet of Jesus. Head knowledge is not true growth, and usually gets in the way. There is no mathematical formula for the abundant life. You can pray and read your Bible all day and still be religious, dry and empty. Jesus is the abundant life. Open to Him. Be filled with Him.

Stay at the feet of the Lord Jesus Christ. Never put your hope in men and never put your hope in the church alone. ***People will almost always disappoint you. We are all terribly weak.*** Don't expect too much from people or you'll live a life full of disappointment. Love people, serve them, and earn the right to speak into their lives by investing in them. Christ is all you've got. He is your source. And although He has called us to be in community with others, Christ is all you need. As you live humbly, needy, dependant, and in regular communion with the Lord Jesus, you will be strengthened in the inner man. You will consistently have hope and encouragement for each day. As you are abiding in the vine, not only will you always be content and satisfied with Christ in you, but you will be well suited for body life, and have something to contribute to those around you.

Personal Help Available

If you would like personal help, I would like to make myself available to your group. I would be happy to come to your city (at my expense) and spend a weekend, an entire week, or more if need be.

Groups tend to fall into one of these three categories of focus which are:

1. Experiential.

2. Cranial/philosophical.

3. Social.

As long as these are of the Spirit and are Biblically based, there is nothing wrong with any one, in and of itself. God does want us to love him with our minds. He wants us to experience Him. And he wants us sharing life together in community. However, we ought to have all three. And all three should be pure, edifying to the body, and scripturally founded.

Many groups are not real sure what to do when they come together. Traditional methods are so a part of our thinking, that many times groups tend to default to passivity in many areas. In so many places meetings are very dry, the presence of the Lord is often not found, vulnerability, intimacy in the Spirit, and a full and powerful expression of consistent body life is extremely rare. In many other places where meetings do not seem to be "dry", emotionalism and soulish manifestations are present which are rarely founded in Biblical truth.

It is always so much better and more effective if you can experience and taste of what to do and how to do it, rather than just reading about it. I definitely do not have all the answers, but perhaps I can be of some help. If I come to help you, I will be working with you and showing you how, instead of just teaching and talking about it.

The Lord has used me in the past to help groups with things like:

- Establishing a foundation in your group which is from the seed of Christ.
- Proper relating to one another and resolving conflicts.
- Troubleshooting where things are off and how to get back on track.
- Quality and freedom in worship.
- Corporate prayer.
- Men leading their families.
- Meeting with the Lord as center.
- Sharing life with one another.
- Personal experience of the Lord.
- Upholding the authority of the scriptures.
- Operating in your spiritual gifts.
- How to pray-read the scriptures together and apply it to your life.
- Parenting issues.
- Undoing traditional church teaching.
- Learning and teaching one another through group discussion.
- Vulnerability and intimacy with God and with one another.

I will be happy to come no matter how small or large your group may be. I will also come whether you are in a traditional church setting or a house church setting. If you are interested, send me an email and we can talk more about it.

To order more copies of this book or to correspond, go to:

www.newtestamentchurchlife.com

This book is the first in a series.

Look for future books coming from Terry Stanley which include:

" *Quality and Passion in Your Personal Life with Jesus*"

" *Being A Man of God In Your Household and in Leading the Church*"

" *How Western Culture Has Infected the Church*"

www.ingramcontent.com/pod-product-compliance
Lightning Source LLC
Chambersburg PA
CBHW031836090426
42741CB00005B/260